University of Michigan Business School Management Series

INNOVATIVE SOLUTIONS TO THE PRESSING PROBLEMS OF BUSINESS

The mission of the University of Michigan Business School Management Series is to provide accessible, practical, and cutting-edge solutions to the most critical challenges facing business-people today. The UMBS Management Series provides concepts and tools for people who seek to make a significant difference in their organizations. Drawing on the research and experience of faculty at the University of Michigan Business School, the books are written to stretch thinking while providing practical, focused, and innovative solutions to the pressing problems of business.

Also available in the UMBS series:

Becoming a Better Value Creator, by Anjan V. Thakor

Achieving Success Through Social Capital, by Wayne Baker

Improving Customer Satisfaction, Loyalty, and Profit, by Michael D. Johnson and Anders Gustafsson

The Compensation Solution, by John E. Tropman

Strategic Interviewing, by Richaurd Camp, Mary Vielhaber, and Jack L. Simonetti

Creating the Multicultural Organization, by Taylor Cox

Getting Results, by Clinton O. Longenecker and Jack L. Simonetti

A Company of Leaders, by Gretchen M. Spreitzer and Robert E. Quinn

Managing the Unexpected, by Karl Weick and Kathleen Sutcliffe

Using the Law for Competitive Advantage, by George J. Siedel

Creativity at Work, by Jeff DeGraff and Katherine A. Lawrence

For additional information on any of these titles or future titles in the series, visit www.umbsbooks.com.

Executive Summary

nformation technologies (I/T) afford clear opportunities to dramatically improve business processes both within and between companies. To date, however, investments in I/T to revamp, reposition, restructure, and resize corporations have generally had limited success. A wide gap persists between the visionary strategies that companies nominally pursue and the operating performance they actually achieve.

This book will help you to close the gap between aspirations and success. Based on a sound, broad framework for management but with special attention to information technology, it will help you to reconsider the nature of business transformation projects and will show you how to root out the causes of implementation failures.

Dramatic improvement in company performance requires equally dramatic changes to business processes and management practices. Today this in turn calls for sizable investments in I/T. However, a company cannot simply invest in technology and expect that business processes will somehow adapt naturally to the new infrastructure. Powerful obstacles conspire to block the initiation of strategic change, to derail its execution once begun, and to frustrate the achievement of its business objectives.

Successful strategic transformation requires a plan based on a strong sense of objective and a credible assessment of current realities. It requires a strategy with specific measures of achievement and unambiguous accountabilities. Success often demands changes in organization and governance structures, as well as investments in new firm competencies and employee skills. It·calls for the commitment of significant amounts of resources and, most important, for the management confidence to launch a bold journey of change and to then adapt plans and adjust schedules as events unfold.

This book provides the basis for the success of such a journey. At its heart is a framework for managing I/T investment opportunities and for overcoming obstacles. The framework consists of two models: the *Business Architecture Model* describes the dimensions in which a business and its operations might change as a result of strategic choices. The *Journey Management Model* identifies the sequence of key activities that take place as a company makes the transition to a new business architecture. The journey model includes a set of some fifty questions as part of a guide and roadmap for leading a program of strategic change.

Chapter One introduces the general challenge and reviews a number of successes and failures. Chapter Two presents the framework. Chapters Three through Six apply the models to a detailed hypothetical case based on actual facts and events from ten corporate research sites in North America, Europe, and Asia. The composite case succinctly presents the situations, issues, and dilemmas that we often uncovered at the research locations. Its unfolding story provides a basis for problem diagnosis and management prescription using the framework. Chapter Seven gives concluding advice.

Making I/T Work

An Executive's Guide to
Implementing Information
Technology Systems

Dennis G. Severance
Jacque Passino

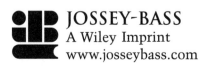

JOSSEY-BASS
A Wiley Imprint
www.josseybass.com

Published by Jossey-Bass
A Wiley Imprint
989 Market Street, San Francisco, CA 94103-1741   www.josseybass.com

Jossey-Bass books and products are available through most bookstores. To contact
Jossey-Bass directly call our Customer Care Department within the U.S. at 800-956-7739,
outside the U.S. at 317-572-3986 or fax 317-572-4002.

Jossey-Bass also publishes its books in a variety of electronic formats. Some content
that appears in print may not be available in electronic books.

Library of Congress Cataloging-in-Publication Data

Severance, Dennis G.
  Making I/T work : an executive's guide to implementing information
technology systems / Dennis G. Severance, Jacque Passino.
    p. cm.— (University of Michigan Business School management
series)
  ISBN 0-7879-6384-4
 1. Information resources management. 2. Information
technology—Management. I. Passino, Jacque. II. Title. III. Series.
  T58.64 .S48 2002
  004'.068'4—dc21

                                                2002009463

Printed in the United States of America
FIRST EDITION
HB Printing   10 9 8 7 6 5 4 3 2

Contents

Series Foreword

Welcome to the University of Michigan Business School Management Series. The books in this series address the most urgent problems facing business today. The series is part of a larger initiative at The University of Michigan Business School (UMBS) that ties together a range of efforts to create and share knowledge through conferences, survey research, interactive and distance training, print publications, and new media.

It is just this type of broad-based initiative that sparked my love affair with UMBS in 1984. From the day I arrived I was enamored with the quality of the research, the quality of the MBA program, and the quality of the Executive Education Center. Here was a business school committed to new lines of research, new ways of teaching, and the practical application of ideas. It was a place where innovative thinking could result in tangible outcomes.

The UMBS Management Series is one very important outcome, and it has an interesting history. It turns out that every year five thousand participants in our executive program fill out a marketing survey in which they write statements indicating the most important problems they face. One day Lucy Chin, one of our administrators, handed me a document containing all these statements. A content analysis of the data resulted in a list of forty-five pressing problems. The topics ranged from growing a company to managing personal stress. The list covered a wide territory, and I started to see its potential. People in organizations tend to be driven by a very traditional set of problems, but the solutions evolve. I went to my friends at Jossey-Bass to discuss a publishing project. The discussion eventually grew into the University of Michigan Business School Management Series—Innovative Solutions to the Pressing Problems of Business.

The books are independent of each other, but collectively they create a comprehensive set of management tools that cut across all the functional areas of business—from strategy to human resources to finance, accounting, and operations. They draw on the interdisciplinary research of the Michigan faculty. Yet each book is written so a serious manager can read it quickly and act immediately. I think you will find that they are books that will make a significant difference to you and your organization.

Robert E. Quinn, Consulting Editor
M.E. Tracy Distinguished Professor
University of Michigan Business School

Preface

This book is based on more than fifty years' experience with new information technologies (I/T). The authors have participated in or advised dozens of companies that were attempting to transform themselves through programs that relied heavily on innovative I/T—and, too often, those programs ended in disappointment. Our common experience has been like that of Bill Murray in the movie *Ground Hog Day*. In the midst of an I/T program review, we've found ourselves thinking, "I've been *here* before! These folks are about to make the same decision that didn't work the last time it was tried! How can I warn them? How can I convince them to stop and reconsider the choice they're about to make?"

What emerged from several years of discussion between us, as colleagues and friends, was the idea that led to this book. Why not record the histories of typical I/T programs—the initial facts of the situation, the sequence of subsequent events, the choices considered and made, and the outcomes that eventually resulted? If such a compendium of histories were available, one could review them later whenever a comparable situation developed. Armed with this knowledge, one could know in advance when disaster was about to strike—and possibly avoid it through some alternative course of action.

Our original plan for this book was simple: First, by synthesizing existing literature on I/T program management, we would construct a nominal framework to describe how a journey of corporate change should proceed under ideal conditions. Second, we'd leverage the contacts that we'd developed over the years to gain access into a representative set of research sites. Third, in visits to these sites, we'd document actual examples of large I/T programs—both those that succeeded and those that didn't. Fourth, we'd use our ideal framework to critique the decisions made in these programs. And finally, if things went as scripted, the framework would allow us to predict the outcomes of decisions made in these I/T efforts, and we could explain how the programs could have been planned and managed better.

Well, no one ever welcomes an audit. In retrospect our plan was naive. It's always easier to second-guess a decision days, weeks, or months later than to make it at the time. During an extended journey of strategic change, more often than not, the unpredictable happens. Factors that no one could foresee and that may never have been very clearly analyzed force choices that no one really wanted. To truly understand why a particular choice was made at a particular time, sometimes you just had to be there.

In the past two years, we conducted dozens of probing conversations with executives and managers who had made large investments in strategic I/T programs. Not all investments had been well planned and prepared for, and even for those that were, not everything had gone smoothly. Although it was difficult to get the participants to speak frankly about their experiences, with the help of strict confidentiality agreements we eventually gathered data from ten large corporations headquartered in North America, Europe, and Asia.

The confidentiality agreements have led us to share the essence of our company interviews in the form of a single composite story: the case of Global Manufacturing Incorporated (GMI). Throughout this book, the story of this hypothetical corporation combines actual facts and events from our interviews. This composite case suffers some loss of face validity, but it offers the advantage of succinct presentation of situations, issues, and dilemmas that recurred at our research sites.

Chapter One offers a brief introduction to the GMI case and its impact on the career of GMI's CEO. The chapter also provides examples of the benefits that can be achieved by an information-enabled corporation, as well as examples to show the obstacles to attaining those benefits. It includes the results of a study of these issues with 280 senior managers from around the globe.

Chapter Two introduces the concepts, providing a framework for understanding and managing organizational change, and it establishes a vocabulary for the remainder of the book. The framework consists of two models. The Business Architecture Model describes the dimensions in which a business and its operations might change as a result of strategic choices. The Journey Management Model defines the sequence of activities that should be followed to accomplish these changes. These models provide a vocabulary and context for examining what is taking place, stage by stage, in the case of GMI.

Prepared by this structure, the next four chapters describe and analyze in detail the strategic journey of change that took place within GMI during the period from 1997 through 2002. We use the unfolding story to diagnose problems and compare how they were and could have been handled. We use it also to demonstrate in detail how the models in Chapter Two can help you to navigate corporate change. Chapter Seven presents our conclusions and offers specific advice for general managers who are either planning or currently involved in an I/T systems initiative in support of a business strategy.

■ Acknowledgments

This book would not have been possible without help from a lot of people. We thank our many colleagues, friends, and clients who have helped us over the past two years to shape and refine our ideas and to conduct our research. We gained particular insight from the professional experiences of these individuals: M. S. Krishnan, Jack Muckstadt, Bill Schmidt, Robert Scott, Howard Selland, and Andrea Weel. In addition, we are grateful for the constructive feedback we received on selected chapters from our reviewers: Gary Whittington of Equilon; Bert Althaver, CEO of Walbro Manufacturing; Randy Muck, partner, Accenture; Ray Perry, CIO of Pitney Bowes; Melanie Kalmar, Dow Chemical; and Neil Nelson, president of Clarkston.

We also are deeply indebted to Accenture, which funded the early research and allowed us to use the Accenture Business Integration Methodology as a basis for the formulation of the models we use extensively in this book.

We would like to thank the Jossey-Bass team, especially Cedric Crocker, Byron Schneider, and Kathe Sweeney, for their suggestions and support in framing the manuscript. We are particularly grateful to Alan Venable for his gifted editing of our original manuscript and insightful suggestions for an improved organization of the book.

Most important, we would like to thank our spouses Camille and Pamela, whose gentle but continued prodding to get our thoughts onto paper kept the writing of this book from slipping forever onto the back burner.

July 2002

Dennis G. Severance
Ann Arbor, Michigan

Jacque Passino
Houston, Texas

Making I/T Work

The Promise and Challenge of I/T Investment

After nearly twenty-five years of nonstop funding for technology, many companies have achieved limited results. Technology investments intended to improve margins, tighten customer relationships, and enable greater synchronization of the supply chain have not lived up to expectations. Few companies have realized this promise. The ones that have, such as General Electric, Cisco, and Dell, are touted heavily in the media. Hardware and software vendors build on their accomplishments, creating an atmosphere that equates buying technology with buying success.

The potential of new information technology is real. However, creating results involves more than buying new software, hardware, and networks. It requires addressing issues that, when overlooked, can turn an investment into an expenditure. The distinction is important—hundreds of companies have spent billions of dollars on new technology with limited results. Companies need approaches that address the issues that impede the ability of technology-enabled change to create new levels of business performance.

We have conducted an in-depth study of 280 senior managers from companies around the world participating in the University of Michigan's Executive Program. The study concentrated on understanding the impediments to implementing information technology and quantifying the business potential of successful technology enabled change. Their input and a review of leading and lagging companies have helped define a framework and leading practices for managing the root causes of failures in technology-led change. They have helped us define the approaches for implementing technology investments that deliver on your company's aspirations and strategies.

Modern business and technology are intertwined to the extent that running a modern company in all of its complexity and scale would be impossible without information technology. This relationship is so close that every major investment in information technology should be considered a project that is transforming your business. Most executives do not understand the connection and leave technology compartmentalized within the I/T department with disastrous effects. Consider the following extract from the case of Global Manufacturing Incorporated (GMI), the fictionalized company we use as a unifying story throughout this book.

■ Brett Berger's Last Days at GMI

Brett Berger, the CEO of Global Manufacturing Incorporated (GMI), was accustomed to being the first to arrive at his office. But on the morning of September 5, 2002, William Browning, the chairman of GMI's Compensation Committee, was waiting for him. Not a man to mince words, Browning got straight to the point. After five years of disappointing corporate performance, the board had lost confidence in Berger's ability to lead GMI back to the forefront of its industry. Of particular concern was Berger's failure to anticipate and plan for the impact that the Internet would have on major GMI customers and thus the absence of I/T capabilities to support their needs. The board would announce Berger's resignation as CEO that afternoon after the close of trading.

The board presumed that Berger would act to facilitate a smooth transition of leadership to the new CEO. If so, all the financial commitments of his current contract would be honored and a generous severance package had been arranged. Thus it was that Brett George Berger, who had struggled tirelessly over the past six years directing a $2 billion program of strategic change by pouring his life and energies into GMI, found himself suddenly unemployed.

Although startled by the delivery of the news, Berger was not completely surprised by the decision. GMI's stock price had dropped precipitously six months before, amid Wall Street rumors that "accounting irregularities" uncovered by external auditors would delay the company's filing of its first quarter financial results. A crash conversion of GMI's information systems infrastructure, designed to provide Internet connectivity to GMI's major customers, had led instead to a breakdown of GMI's accounting controls. A failure to accurately record manufacturing expenses had inflated the profit guidance provided to financial analysts in March and profits for the quarter were 35 percent below what Wall Street had expected.

A thorough audit of the GMI's books would eventually reveal innocent but material accounting problems. As inbound shipments had arrived at GMI plants during the first quarter of 2002, new software had rejected hundreds of receipt transactions for coding errors. Production work releases then locked up because of the apparent lack of these raw materials, which were actually on site. A subsequent series of "creative" shop floor actions designed to work around the new system had thrown GMI's production operations into chaos. Manual releases of the production orders initially kept the factory busy, but then without shipment receipts suppliers went unpaid and new purchase orders went unissued. Eventually materials failed to arrive, production faltered, orders were cancelled, and customer accounts were lost. The new $106 million I/T infrastructure designed to provide Internet access to GMI's business applications simply did not work as planned.

Despite the best efforts of the GMI management team, it took nearly six months to untangle the mess and to correct the operating and accounting problems, with predictable impact on the company's stock price. Today the stock stood at less than 60 percent of its value in January 2002. Institutional investors were clamoring for a change of leadership and a concrete turn-around plan. Brett Berger was a natural casualty of these events.

By the next afternoon, Berger had resigned himself to the loss of his job and was pleasantly surprised by the feeling of freedom that he was suddenly enjoying. After years of explaining disappointing corporate performance, it was now a relief to let go of the responsibility. He would retire at age fifty-six, four years earlier than planned, but the board had left him financially well off. He could finally get to work on improving his golf game, and there was a new grandson that he was looking forward to spending some time with. As he now sat alone in a GMI conference room fielding phone calls from the business press, he stuck closely to the scripted explanation for his departure.

"The board and I have agreed that the time has come for a dramatic change in our business strategy and that it would make most sense to implement this new strategy with new leadership. I have therefore asked to step down as CEO immediately, but will make myself

available as needed during a transition period to provide assistance and advice as it might make sense to the new CEO."

Actually, Brett Berger had no clue as to what this dramatic change in business strategy might be, nor could he imagine what he could have done differently during his tenure of the past six years. He had applied well-tested management processes to direct the strategic turnaround at GMI. He had recruited seasoned management, hired experienced consultants, formed a cross-functional transition team, developed strategic plans, and invested heavily in modern technologies. Yet despite the dedication of his long hours and the commitment of substantial resources by the company, these processes had failed to bring GMI back to industry leadership. Either there had been something fundamentally different in the organizational resistance that had confronted him over the past six years or, as concluded by the board, there was something lacking in his leadership.

Your Analysis

Before you read on, think a few moments about what you've just read.

1. How is it possible for an executive like Brett Berger of GMI to be blindsided by the business implications of an emerging technology such as the Internet?
2. How could this strategic change process have gotten so badly out of control if, as described, Berger had "recruited seasoned managers, developed strategic plans, and hired experienced consultants"?

■ Unmet Expectations of I/T Investment

The GMI story will be laid out in detail in later chapters. The story is an object lesson in the difficulty of radically changing an established company by using technology as the leading wedge.

It also provides a basis for demonstrating how the difficulties can be overcome.

As corporations have taken their first steps into the twenty-first century, one cannot help but be struck by the promise of a newly emerging form of information-enabled enterprise. There lies before us the possibility of dramatic improvements in product quality, customer service, and market innovation, with simultaneous reductions in capital investment and operating expenses. The confusion, disappointment, and waste caused by ineffective communication between a firm and its supply chain partners can soon be eliminated. The delay between recognition of a customer need and the development of reliable and cost-effective products that satisfy that need can be compressed. The velocity with which raw materials are delivered by suppliers and transformed into final products can be accelerated. The collection of information, the codification of expertise, and the sharing of knowledge can revolutionize the processes of business and the delivery of customer service. Organizational layers can be removed and executives can have greater touch with their customers. At the same time employees can have more autonomy and authority to accomplish their tasks. We are witnessing the genesis of a new form of information-enabled corporation whose internal and external operating characteristics are summarized in Figure 1.1.

Information technology—the combination of data capture, storage, indexing, retrieval, computing, and telecommunication—has evolved as a potent catalyst for the creation of a new form of business enterprise by moving global supply chains toward a single tightly integrated system. The ability to communicate globally is available today, but also becoming faster and more reliable with the installation of high-bandwidth networks that allow instantaneous transmission of large amounts of data at affordable prices. The emergence of standard hardware and software platforms coupled with standards for business data capture and exchange in

External Supply-Chain Operations

- Accelerated development of products for market segments
- Trusted and leveraged supplier partnerships
- Tightly integrated, high-velocity production
- Finished products of ship-to-use quality
- Rapid, on-time–every-time delivery
- Global markets and manufacturing

Internal Business Operations

- Wider span of employee involvement and influence
- Common databases and accessible information
- Fewer layers: faster, clearer communication
- Decentralized authority and decision making
- Computer-based agents and expertise
- Centralized monitoring and control
- Blurred functional boundaries

Figure 1.1. Operating Characteristics of an Information-Enabled Company.

the form of standard enterprise resource planning (ERP) systems have made powerful and robust business processes affordable to companies of all sizes. Data of all types—numbers, text, drawings, photos, voice, and video—can now be digitized, stored, processed, and exchanged among modestly priced computers located throughout an industry's supply chain.

A Few Recent Successes

Consider two major corporations that have succeeded through I/T investments.

Dell Uses Technology to Communicate
with Customers and Coordinate with Suppliers
In April 2000, the Dell Computer Corporation claimed the position of the number one computer systems company in the United States and number two worldwide. The company generated $25 billion in revenues in 1999, with more than half coming from online sales. Dell, which launched its first Web site in

1994 and initiated online sales in 1996, has been a longtime leader in commercialization of the Internet. Today it operates one of the highest-volume Internet commerce sites in the world. Customer visits to consider, configure, price, purchase, and track delivery of orders exceeded 35 million in the fourth quarter of 1999. Dell sells $40 million worth of computers from its Web site each day. About 90 percent of Dell's overall sales are to institutional accounts and 70 percent of its sales are to accounts larger than $1 million per year.

The Internet has proven an ideal match with Dell's direct marketing approach. Dell uses this system not only to sell computers but also to reduce its own operating costs while it improves customer service. The Web site's main weapon is the Premier Page program, which serves the largest of Dell's forty thousand corporate, government, and education accounts worldwide. When Dell wins a corporate customer with more than four hundred employees, it will build that customer a Premier Page. The Premier Page is a set of smaller Web pages, often linked to the customer's intranet, that let approved employees go online to configure PCs, pay for them, and track their delivery status. More than $30 million of Dell systems are ordered this way each business day. After the sale, Premier Pages provide access to instant technical support and Dell sales representatives when needed.

Because Dell's suppliers also have real-time access to information about current orders via Dell's extranet, they can coordinate their production and delivery to ensure that Dell has just enough of the right parts to keep the production line moving smoothly. By plugging its suppliers directly into its customer database, Dell ensures that they will instantly know about any changes in demand. And by also plugging its customers into its supply chain via its Web site, Dell enables them to track the progress of their orders from the factory to their doorstep, thus saving on telephone or fax inquiries.

Such fast, affordable, ubiquitous real-time access to shared information has been fueled by dramatic improvements in underlying information technologies, which capture, store, index, retrieve, transform, and transmit data. Moore's Law, which has been at the heart of these advances, observes that smaller, lighter, faster, cheaper computing processes and storage devices emerge at a rate that doubles capabilities (or halves costs) every eighteen months. Local and worldwide networking capability, coupled with ample and relatively inexpensive bandwidth, allows for the movement of data from the places where it is created to the places where it can be put to use. The resultant reduction in transaction costs between buyers and sellers in the supply chain has given rise to new business models. In addition, the ease of access to significantly more relevant information has given rise to substantially better management decisions.

Cisco Uses Technology to Transform Its Business Model
Cisco Systems is famous for selling its complex routers and networking equipment over the World Wide Web. Customers place their orders through its Web site and suppliers know exactly what materials and components they need to ship to the factory by accessing Cisco's dynamic replenishment software through a Web interface. Internet applications reach into every part of the company's operation. With the online pricing and configuration tools, about 98 percent of the orders go through Cisco's system the first time, saving time both at Cisco and at the customer site. The average lead times for orders have dropped by several days, and customer's productivity increased an average of 20 percent per order.

When the company was faced with the problem of growing faster than it was capable of handling, it took its solution to the Web. Cisco was being bombarded by numerous technical support calls about its systems and it didn't have the manpower to answer customer questions and get the orders out. Cisco decided to put as much of its support as possible online so that customers would be able to resolve most workaday problems on their own, leaving Cisco's own engineers free to assist with the most difficult problems.

Today, Cisco's customers and reseller partners log onto Cisco's Web site more than 900,000 times a month to receive technical assistance, check orders, or download software. The online service has been so well received that more than 80 percent of customer and partner queries are answered online.

With an estimated 70 percent of its technical support and customer service calls handled online, Cisco's technical support productivity has increased by 200–300 percent, translating to roughly $125 million lower technical support staff costs each year. Customers download new software releases directly from Cisco's site, saving the company $180 million in distribution, packaging, and duplication costs. Having product and pricing information on the Web and Web-based CD-ROMs saves Cisco an additional $50 million on printing and distributing catalogs and marketing materials to customers.

It is further estimated that Cisco saves $37 million each year by providing employee services over the company's intranet. For travel expense reimbursement, for example, it takes just two staff members to administer and audit the filings of seventeen thousand employees. Total estimates indicate that putting applications online saved Cisco $680 million in 1999, or approximately 14 percent of its actual operating costs.

A Well-Publicized Failure

In preparation for this new business game of tightly integrated global supply chains, most large corporations have been redesigning their information infrastructures. Many have already invested heavily in the technology required to support an information-enabled enterprise: personal computers for white-collar productivity; networks, intranets, and extranets for interorganizational communications; and ERP systems to standardize data definitions and connect business processes across functions and geographic locations. But simply investing in new technologies such as computer hardware and ERP software has not guaranteed desirable business outcomes—you need to change business processes as well as organization and governance practices in order to take advantage of it.

Hershey Foods Has Implementation Problems with Its ERP System
In mid-1996, Hershey Foods was saddled with computer systems that were not yet Year-2000 compliant and faced with retailers who were demanding more fine-tuned, just-in-time store deliveries. The nation's largest candy maker (with revenues in the billions) embarked upon an ERP investment in excess of $100 million. Its new computer system was designed to automate and modernize nearly all of Hershey's business processes. When completed, the new systems were to support setting prices, taking orders, managing raw materials, planning production, loading trucks, scheduling delivery, billing for orders, and assessing the effectiveness of marketing campaigns. Just as the large demand for Halloween candy was arriving in July 1999, the entire system went live. Within weeks customers realized that something was wrong. Deliveries from this historically reliable supplier failed to arrive and accurate information on the status of orders was unavailable. Hershey still had ample manufacturing capacity and inventories to serve its accounts, but it appeared to have lost the handle on its order processing and distribution activities. Its people simply could not get the candy through their warehouses to their customers on time. These problems contributed to a loss of share to Mars and Nestlé, and by February 2000 the stock price had fallen by a third.

A Surer Road to Heaven

The Hershey saga is not unique. Our interviews with executives from dozens of other companies suggest that many more are talking about heaven than are actually getting there. Widely reported problems at Whirlpool, Macys, and Toys-R-Us suggest that sizable investments in I/T infrastructure alone will not guarantee favorable business results. To reap the benefits enabled by new infrastructure, the general manager will first need to direct a planning process that critically assesses the firm's business model and challenges the fundamental assumptions under which it currently operates.

1. To assure a successful transformation, the general manager must first lead a formulation process that will
   - Establish the need for change to remain competitive in the emerging world of business.
   - Define a shared vision of what the enterprise is to become and how it will get there.

2. With the purpose established, the general manager must direct preparation processes that will
   - Define the business capabilities required to implement the shared vision.
   - Develop a plan to make the investments and implement the actions needed to build the new business capabilities.

3. With a plan in hand, the general manager must assure success of an implementation process that will
   - Manage the program and project activities necessary to achieve the planned capabilities.
   - Harvest the value promised by the strategic vision in a planned and proactive manner.

In Chapter Two we will provide more details on this step-by-step approach. First, however, it's useful to identify the variety of business goals that might justify an investment in a new business processes and information infrastructure—and also the obstacles that arise in practice and conspire to block the initiation of strategic changes based upon these investments.

■ Business Goals of Information Technology Investments

In our study of technology-enabled strategic change, we inquired as to the nature of the process improvements that the managers' firms could most benefit from as a result of an information technology investment, if there were no impediments to implementing such changes. Figure 1.2 synthesizes the responses of our 280 executives into four categories of opportunities for benefit:

- Improve existing processes within the firm.
- Improve existing processes between firms.
- Establish new practices within the firm.
- Establish new practices between firms.

The two lists shown on the left of the figure contain the changes designed to improve existing processes of the business. Here the managers described enhancements both to operations within their own firm and to interactions their firm had with partners, suppliers, customers, or consumers. The two lists shown on the right of the figure focus on the potential to establish new practices for conducting business operations both internally and externally.

Improve Existing Processes Within the Firm: Tenneco

Internal opportunities ranged from increased productivity improvements based on process automation to process standardization based on shared best practices across locations. Respondents described the potential value of standard data definitions and

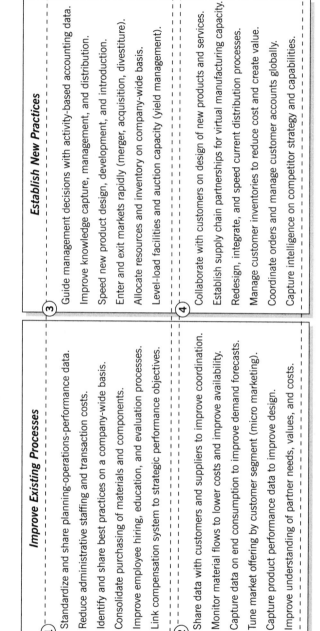

Figure 1.2. Business Goals of Information System Initiatives.

Improve Existing Processes

(1)
- Standardize and share planning-operations-performance data.
- Reduce administrative staffing and transaction costs.
- Identify and share best practices on a company-wide basis.
- Consolidate purchasing of materials and components.
- Improve employee hiring, education, and evaluation processes.
- Link compensation system to strategic performance objectives.

(2)
- Share data with customers and suppliers to improve coordination.
- Monitor material flows to lower costs and improve availability.
- Capture data on end consumption to improve demand forecasts.
- Tune market offering by customer segment (micro marketing).
- Capture product performance data to improve design.
- Improve understanding of partner needs, values, and costs.

Establish New Practices

(3)
- Guide management decisions with activity-based accounting data.
- Improve knowledge capture, management, and distribution.
- Speed new product design, development, and introduction.
- Enter and exit markets rapidly (merger, acquisition, divestiture).
- Allocate resources and inventory on company-wide basis.
- Level-load facilities and auction capacity (yield management).

(4)
- Collaborate with customers on design of new products and services.
- Establish supply chain partnerships for virtual manufacturing capacity.
- Redesign, integrate, and speed current distribution processes.
- Manage customer inventories to reduce cost and create value.
- Coordinate orders and manage customer accounts globally.
- Capture intelligence on competitor strategy and capabilities.

Within a Firm

Between Firms

common databases for coordinated market planning, for consolidated materials purchasing, for rational resource allocation, and for optimal process execution. They also observed the opportunity to drive cooperative behavior among employees with a clear linkage between individual compensation and team performance. Finally, better information offered chances to improve the processes for recruiting, developing, and retaining employees.

Tenneco Automotive monitors improvements in process by tracking performance in real time. Tenneco employs an accounting system of key indicators called its Business Operating System to guide management choices and to monitor performance of employees ranging from business unit heads to shop floor workers. At each level, four to ten measures with clear linkage to the business unit strategy are used to monitor and reward performance. In addition, the system allows the linkage of labor, overhead, and material costs to the variety of specific products that pour through the company's plants on a given day. This permits Tenneco's management to maintain a handle on those products and customers from whom they make and lose money, so that they can make more informed pricing decisions.

Improve Existing Processes Between Firms: Cisco

Efficiency improvements between firms derive from the open sharing of information with customers, suppliers, and other business partners. Mutual understanding of business objectives, marketing plans, and production capabilities allows for more informed allocations of capacity, inventory, and human resources before orders are transacted. Monitoring of actual sales and materials movements allows for improvements in capacity utilization, inventory investment, and product availability once production begins. And finally, a better understanding of current product performance and evolving needs, values, and costs of supply-chain partners provides a basis for improving the next iteration of the product offerings or supply-chain design.

Cisco has taken the concept of collaboration with suppliers to new heights, reducing investment through collaboration. It owns only two of the thirty-four plants that manufacture its product components, and more than fifty percent of its product orders are filled without Cisco employees being directly involved. Consider, for example, Cisco's relationship with Flextronics, one of a growing breed of electronic manufacturing services (EMS) providers. Between 1996 and 2000 the annual revenues of EMS providers worldwide more than doubled, to $88 billion. As traditional manufacturers have downsized and focused on core competencies, EMS providers have slipped in to fill a profitable manufacturing niche. Unlike traditional manufacturers, EMS companies do not make their own brand name products, they provide production and sometimes engineering and design services to all comers. Their factories are designed to be quickly rearranged so that they can provide different products to many different customers. Through electronic integration they provide rapid, just-in-time delivery while holding minimal inventories. They have a sharp focus on making products without any worry about heavy R&D and marketing. They can obtain cheaper components than their customers can by buying in mass quantities. While gross margins run at a relatively modest 6–8 percent, the low overhead structure that they enjoy yields comfortable RONAs of 15–25 percent. Flextronics revenues have grown from $100 million in 1993 to more than $2 billion today.

Establish New Practices Within the Firm: Dell

Those innovations most frequently cited as desired new internal practices included the ability to judge the profitability of existing products, processes, and customers, the capability to speed new product introduction, and the confidence to enter or exit a market faster. Important was the ability to allocate and share capacity, inventory, and personnel on a firmwide basis, and also the development of the management sophistication needed to participate in newly emerging Web-based production planning and auction processes that promise to improve the yield from existing production capacity.

The success of Dell Computer's reliance on its very capable management accounting data system is illustrated by the story of the company's love-hate relationship with the consumer market. Dell made an abortive foray into the retail business in 1989, fearing that its direct sales model alone might not sustain the revenue growth that was needed for long-term profitability. By closely monitoring its costs to serve that segment of the business, however, it was quick to recognize that the rock-bottom prices demanded by superstores and warehouse clubs could not support its profit objectives. It was thus able to exit that market relatively quickly. It did not actively pursue the sales-support–intensive consumer segment of the direct sales business again for seven years. Eventually, it was able to detect that its direct-to-consumer segment had slowly shifted from first-time buyers who required a lot of handholding to computer-savvy customers who were upgrading their homes with top-of-the-line equipment. The segment had grown to a billion-dollar business that was now quite profitable. Dell then decided it was time to dedicate a group to serving the consumer segment aggressively.

Establish New Practices Between Firms: Procter & Gamble

Attractive new practices linking firms in a supply chain included collaborating with customers in the design of new products, partnering with suppliers to create virtual manufacturing capacity, managing customer inventories to obtain real-time data on product consumption, capturing competitive intelligence to anticipate market shifts, sharing plans with partners to enable collaboration, and finally establishing an informed basis upon which to identify and design customized offerings for new market segments.

Procter & Gamble has begun innovative collaboration with consumers. P&G now offers custom-blended, state-of-the-art skin care, hair care, and makeup products for which it can charge a premium price. Its Internet venture, Reflect.com, invites customers into an online studio to custom design thousands of different formulations and to custom package them as well. The final product is then delivered directly to the consumer, thereby bypassing the traditional distribution channel.

A Combination of Missed Opportunities?

In combination, the business improvement opportunities described here offer the benefits of lower cost, expanded market, and economies of scale and scope. With such obvious benefits from timely access to accurate information regarding a firm's products, processes, customers, consumers, suppliers, and industry partners, why don't we see a lot more of it?

Unlocking the profit potential captive within these opportunities has proven elusive in practice. A recent study of such change efforts reveals that most information technology–related projects fail to achieve their objectives as planned. Nearly a third of the projects begun are cancelled before completion and only one in ten achieves its original plan. For the remainder, budget and schedule overruns approach 100 percent, while the functionality delivered at the end of the project is less than half of what was originally anticipated. There seems to be some perverse form of Pareto's 80–20 Rule in operation. Companies appear to make the financial commitments necessary to permit shared information to flow throughout their organizations, and yet they seem to extract few of the benefits that could be derived from improved business operations and customer service.

Your Analysis

Before proceeding to read about the obstacles that we have observed between organizations and potential benefits, spend a few moments considering your own awareness of this problem.

1. Do the rather bleak statistics cited here match your own experience? How is it that this might happen?
2. From your own experience, what types of obstacles might block I/T-enabled process innovations from succeeding?

■ Obstacles to Innovation

Many obstacles conspire to impede progress toward the idealized vision of a tightly integrated, global supply chain. Physical distance slows interpersonal communication and adds expense to supply-chain logistics. Time zone and cultural differences complicate attempts at coordination. Local customs, codes, and laws thwart efforts aimed at global standards. Performance measurement systems inhibit intraorganizational cooperation. Incompatible and geographically dispersed hardware and poorly documented software represent a monumental standardization and conversion task. Most important, the organizational structures, management philosophies, and investment justification practices that exist in many organizations today are simply inappropriate to support the degree of change to which organizations aspire. It is to these issues that the focus of general management attention is required if business process change is to be successfully accomplished.

When we asked our sample of 280 executives to describe the obstacles within their own organizations that blocked pursuit of the opportunities summarized in Figure 1.2, they provided literally hundreds of examples, which we synthesized into the four categories shown in Figure 1.3.

1 Company Legacy
Prior choices constrain our current options.

Company culture is inward focused or change resistant.

Existing policies, rules, and regulations inhibit change.

There is distrust among partners who must collaborate.

Systems are incompatible and functionally focused.

We have weak growth processes: technology, education, strategy.

We have little or no experience with large system projects.

2 Required Journey
These changes will be complex or painful.

Very large investment is required for the new systems.

New processes must be designed, learned, and accepted.

Required data is not captured or not likely to be shared.

New skills, people, or partners must be cultivated.

Customers or suppliers will need assistance and subsidy.

We face significant risk of a failure with dire consequences.

3 Current Conditions
This is a bad time for change.

Resources are scarce: time, talent, people, or money.

We have too many options to consider and choices to be made.

Other business initiatives compete for time and resources.

Customer needs and expectations are evolving rapidly.

Technology is evolving: capabilities, security, cost.

I/T expenses are viewed as overhead to be reduced.

4 Lack of Purpose
Why, where, what, and how will we change?

Management is unaware of what is possible or needed.

We have no industry models of collaboration and sharing.

Incentive systems do not encourage experimentation.

We have no business strategy to focus possible innovations.

Specifications of benefits, costs, and schedule are vague.

We have no strong leader to champion the change initiative.

Figure 1.3. Obstacles to Information System Initiatives.

Company Legacy: Auto Dealers

Company legacy is the collection of constraints to action that derive from prior events and management decisions. Ironically, it is often the most successful companies that face the greatest risk of technological obsolescence. During an extended period of business success, process innovation is often discouraged to avoid upsetting a good thing. As a result, organizational processes for renewal (employee development, technology research, and strategy formulation) are permitted to atrophy, and the brightest and most ambitious employees tend to find more exciting opportunities in other companies. Older successful companies may thus find themselves technically and culturally isolated. When times get tough, they suffer the malady of "brand ego," which makes it difficult to look past their prior glory days. When profits dwindle, such companies tend to hunker down and hope to ride out the storm. Management will attempt to cut expenses and conserve capital in an effort to sustain the profit profile that capital markets have come to expect. Capital appropriations become more modest and with a faster payback. As a result, system investments take on a local or functional perspective and focus on cost cutting and working capital reduction. But these investments are inadequate to remain competitive with emerging industry leaders.

A narrow attention to short-term financial performance can have a disastrous effect on a firm's infrastructure. The I/T application portfolio, for example, can deteriorate into a collection of functional process compromises and software patches. It then becomes impossible to evolve such a tangled collection of applications into the systems infrastructure needed to support tightly connected supply-chain operations. To do so, the old systems must be completely replaced, creating a dramatic shock to the central nervous system of the corporation. Such significant process change in turn requires the cooperation and support of the workers, suppliers, distributors, and customers. But for many of these firms, a history of shortsighted cost-cutting initiatives has left a legacy of suspicion and distrust among these parties. Change (if any) comes slowly and in measured increments. This tendency toward conservative, piecemeal adaptation is re-inforced in industries where government regulation, union contracts, or a dominant satisfied customer (or supplier) make radical changes to business models difficult to even discuss. Finally, given the resulting inexperience with large-scale project implementation, it is difficult either to focus sufficient resources within a firm or to generate much enthusiasm for complex projects of high risk and long duration.

Auto dealers use franchise laws to block online purchase of new cars, despite the fact that the current system for selling new cars is notoriously inefficient and accounts for as much as 25 percent of the price of a new automobile. By using the Internet to streamline the process, the consumer could save $1,000 or more on a vehicle, and dealers themselves could cut $800–$1,000 per car in marketing, financing, and sales expense. For decades an information asymmetry has clearly put the dealer in the driver's seat as options, discounts, and financing terms were negotiated. And as a result, car shoppers have relished a trip to a new car dealer with the same enthusiasm as a visit to the dentist. But all of this began to change in the mid-1990s as the Internet made it easy to gather comparative information on the availability, cost, and performance of hundreds of models of various brands of automobiles. Internet sites like Edmunds, Autobytel, and CarsDirect offered consumers a hassle-free way to gather facts about the vehicles that they were about to buy. The average Autobytel customer was found to save $450 on a purchase, while some online shoppers saved $5,000 or more off of the new vehicle list price. During the first quarter of 2000, CarsDirect sold six thousand cars online. Today nearly half of new-car buyers use the Internet to research their purchase and it is projected that 20–30 percent of cars will be sold over the Internet within a few years.

The reaction of the auto industry to all of this has been to stonewall the inevitable with legal maneuvering. The dealers have applied their considerable clout in state legislatures to stiffen franchise laws to prohibit the sale of automobiles by anyone other than an established dealer. Today state regulations generally require that new cars be sold only by dealers who have been licensed and inspected by regulators and specifically bar manufacturers from bypassing their dealers. Thus companies like CarsDirect must obtain their cars from a dealer rather than purchasing directly from automakers in an effort to eliminate unnecessary overhead. And the automakers for their own part have also filed suits reminding the dealers not to do business with Internet brokers.

All this shortsighted protectionism is unlikely to stem the Internet tide. Consumers Union estimates that the current franchise restrictions, which preclude automakers and independent companies alike from selling cars directly over the Internet, costs consumers $20 billion a year. The Consumer Federation of America, a Washington-based coalition of consumer groups, has recently begun a campaign to change state regulations on automobile sales.

Required Journey: General Electric

The phrase *required journey* stands for concerns that the required investment is beyond the resources and stamina of the firm. Enterprise-wide system replacements are large and complex. These projects are likely to be bigger than anything the firm has attempted in terms of scale, scope, financial commitment, business sophistication, and skill requirements. Whereas in the past, process automation projects have often prided themselves on eliminating clerical work while maintaining basic information flows and operating processes, these new projects *must* change existing business practices if they are successful.

New data flows must be created and skills at leveraging this information must be developed. Current employees must be informed regarding the reasons for change and the nature of the impact on them and their operations. Some jobs will be eliminated while others are created. Those employees whose jobs remain must be retrained and supported during the transition. In addition, new talent will be hired and salary scales will shift upward.

All this has significant expense and investment implications, and yet the benefits of the project are uncertain and long-term in nature, since the duration of the journey can be five years or more. New channels of distribution must be developed. Long-term relationships with loyal partners must be redesigned or possibly abandoned. If the relationships are redesigned, these partners may need educational assistance and financial subsidy to make a transition to the new ways of doing business. The journey of business process change will demand careful planning and flawless execution. It is one with the potential to destroy the company if the change is tried and fails.

GE had considerable reluctance to embrace the Internet. For twenty years beginning in the late 1970s, electronic data interchange (EDI) had been the standard for conducting online business-to-business transactions and GE Information Services (GEIS) was the world leader in enabling these interactions. EDI saves money for large companies by speeding business transactions and by eliminating associated clerical costs and errors. With the maturing of the Internet, new business-to-business service companies like Commerce One and Ariba began to provide a business alternative in the form of inexpensive but effective software for conducting electronic commerce over the Internet. This new software not only replaced traditional EDI messaging but also offered new forms of business interaction such as product auctions, markets, and exchanges. These approaches can bypass traditional distribution channels and their expense.

GEIS did not react to this emerging threat to its business. Its staff viewed the Internet merely as an ad hoc alternative to their services for smaller firms that could not afford to establish their own private EDI network and therefore had to opt instead for the public Internet. If GEIS were to attack this small market niche, a considerable investment would be required and success could cannibalize its existing profitable and proprietary business. It faced the classic Innovator's Dilemma.

Nothing changed at GEIS until the year 2000, when Jack Welch, GE's legendary CEO, introduced a process of strategic transformation called Destroy Your Business. His goal was to encourage each of his business units to anticipate the vulnerabilities of its current business model to the threat of the Internet and to reinvent itself before someone else did. Out of that analysis and change process GEIS emerged as two separate businesses: GE System Services, which focused on the traditional GEIS lines of business, and GE Global Exchange Services, a new software and marketplace builder prepared to counter the intrusion by the new competition.

Current Conditions: A Chief Operating Officer

The Current Conditions quadrant of Figure 1.3 reflects concerns that this is an inappropriate moment for a major change of strategic direction. An old Irish joke ends with unsatisfying advice to a lost traveler: "If I wanted to go to Dublin, I would not be planning to leave from here." There is likewise no good place and time to begin radical change to the business practices of a well-established corporation.

Companies most in need of extensive change are often under organizational stress and financial pressure to avoid large investments of time, money, and emotional energy. It is difficult in these companies to justify the expenditure of tens or hundreds of millions of dollars on the overhead of an I/T infrastructure when other more immediate business initiatives are contending for attention and much smaller sums. Often such companies have been embroiled in performance improvement programs and their employees are physically weary and mentally exhausted. Family breakups and nervous breakdowns are not uncommon.

In these situations, people instinctively try to slow the processes of change. Moreover, they have good reasons to proceed with caution. The recent business press is replete with stories of I/T-related operational fiascoes that have misstated financial performance, compromised sensitive customer data, and missed production and delivery commitments. In addition, the technologies that support and enable changes in process continue to grow in capability and drop in price. Likewise, the expectations and demands of customers continue to evolve as industries gather experience with the new applications of data communication and information sharing. Rather than move prematurely with system investments that may soon be obsolete, it seems to make sense to wait and see how things will work out. But companies that succumb to that reasoning are like deer caught in the headlights—the results of their delay can be disastrous.

During our data collection process we interviewed the chief operating officer of an old-line manufacturing firm that had managed to maintain an unbroken string of twenty-nine consecutive quarters of revenue and profit growth. He was psychologically incapable of accepting the financial effects on current earnings that a major Internet infrastructure investment would have on this inherited record of performance. He protested that the company would turn over its entire investor base if he were to invest what was required to renew its information infrastructure. Over the year that followed his failure to act, we watched as the price of this company's stock dropped by nearly two-thirds. The shareholders on their own had observed that the firm was clearly locked into an untenable operating paradigm as new information-enabled competitors rose up around it, and had abandoned it in droves.

Lack of Purpose: A Management Task Force

The Lack of Purpose quadrant collects the debilitating effects of the failure to choose a course of action. The single biggest obstacle to change reported in our interviews was the lack of a compelling description of the future of the company that could be used to explain why, what, where, and how the organization was going to change—a vision that could mobilize the imagination, resources, and energy of the corporation.

This problem is generally evidenced either by the absence of a strong champion for change or by the lack of a strategic plan with clear specification of resource allocations, performance targets, accountabilities, and delivery schedules. As explanation for this state of affairs we learned that top management in some companies were uninformed with respect to what was possible in the emerging world of e-business or simply discounted stories of information sharing and collaboration in other industries as nontransferable to their own. It was common to learn also that incentive systems and bonus structures placed more weight on minimizing budget variances than on encouraging risk taking and innovation. As a result, functional managers stick to doing what they know will work and continue to play the current game as they always have.

A leadership phenomenon documented several times in our study was that of an older management struggling to establish a vision of e-business. To this end, a cadre of bright and energetic managers had been brought together to think creatively about the likely future of their industry and to lead a project of business process change within the corporation. Often these individuals had been previously identified as high-potential employees and specifically selected for the strategic planning project by their executive management. For many this project was a full-time job. Motivated by either external threats to their firm or internal opportunities to improve profits, the team was tasked to work quickly to propose an innovative plan for change. They were challenged to "think outside the box" and to "break the existing rules" as necessary to develop new business models with significant competitive advantages for their firms.

Despite the dedication and best efforts of these teams, their projects generally ended with disappointment. Sometimes the change initiatives aborted for lack of serious executive attention and support; and sometimes these efforts stumbled forward into operation without prerequisite investments in process infrastructure and organizational design. Inevitably, without required resources coupled with powerful leadership, these projects lost traction and disbanded. They fell victim to a lack of appreciation for the dimensions and magnitude of the effort that was being commissioned, and to the unwillingness of executive management to take true ownership of the vision once it had been developed by their team.

Flaws in Management?

The obstacles listed here suggest that the failure to achieve the benefits of technology-enabled change within corporations may have had little to do with the capabilities of the technology itself. Rather, the lack of success may flow from flaws in the management philosophy, strategic planning process, investment justification practices, and performance measurement systems that exist in those organizations.

Your Analysis

Take a few moments here to reflect again.

1. Have you experienced implementation problems with any large-scale investments analogous to those encountered in the preceding sections or reflected in the opening story about Brett Berger at GMI?
2. What similarities or differences do you recognize?

■ The Importance of Planning

The lesson in this book is simple—dramatic improvement in company performance requires equally dramatic changes to business processes and management practices. Today this in turn calls for sizable investments in information technology. However, it is naive to hope of leading a strategic business transformation by investing first in technology and expecting that the business processes will somehow adapt naturally to the new infrastructure. Powerful obstacles conspire both to block the initiation of strategic change and to derail its execution once begun.

Success requires a clear direction—a plan built with a strong sense of business objectives and a realistic assessment of where we begin. It requires a strategy with specific measures of achievement and unambiguous accountabilities. Success is likely to demand changes in organization and governance structures, as well as investments in new firm competencies and employee skills. It calls for the commitment of significant amounts of resources and, most important, for the management confidence to launch a bold journey of change and to then adapt plans and adjust schedules as events unfold. In Chapter Two, we present a framework of organizational transformation that places the problems of change management into a context so that they can be effectively addressed.

The framework consists of two models. The first model describes the dimensions in which a business and its operations might change as a result of strategic choices. The second defines the sequence of activities that must be followed to accomplish these changes most effectively.

On this structure Chapters Three, Four, Five, and Six provide an elaboration and analysis of the Global Manufacturing Incorporated (GMI) story introduced at the start of this chapter. The GMI case is the description of a hypothetical corporation in which actual facts and events from ten corporate research sites have been combined. The composite case offers a succinct presentation of situations, issues, and dilemmas that we uncovered on a recurrent basis at our interview locations. As the story unfolds, it provides a basis for problem diagnosis and management prescription using the models of Chapter Two. Chapter Seven summarizes our insights and recommendations.

SUMMARY

Information technology is a pivotal element in the operations of the emerging twenty-first-century corporation. A well-designed I/T infrastructure will support fast, reliable sharing of planning and operating data. Such sharing can enable new levels of coordination, cooperation, and collaboration activities both within and between firms leading them to improved profitability.

Achieving the potential profits from improved communications has proven elusive in practice. Many obstacles—physical, cultural, and organizational—impede progress toward the idealized vision of a tightly integrated, global supply chain. Success requires a strategic vision with specific measures of achievement and unambiguous accountabilities. Success demands changes in business processes and their supporting infrastructure. It calls for the commitment of significant amounts of resources and, most important, it requires management skill and confidence to take bold steps.

The following chapter provides a framework for directing complex change within an organization and for overcoming the types of obstacles that were described here. Among other things, the framework offers a language with which to clarify the need for, nature of, and goals assigned to strategic I/T investments. It also provides a road map and a set of steps for achieving the purpose of those investments.

Questions for Consideration

Assume for the moment that advances in technology will continue to drive the cost of computing down to the point that the collection, storage, access, and filtering of information is effectively free. Suppose therefore that you could quickly and affordably retrieve accurate information on the plans, performance, or status of your firm's products, processes, customers, consumers, suppliers, and industry partners.

1. What three things would you or your firm do differently in this new environment?
2. What value would be derived from the new capabilities that you have outlined? What would you be willing to pay in order to enjoy these capabilities?
3. Do you believe that the nature of resistance to I/T-based strategic change is fundamentally different in some ways from that depicted in this book thus far? How and why?

2

Managing Organizational Change

How might the GMI story described in Chapter One have turned out differently? How could this failure of an I/T-enabled business transformation have been prevented? What guidance or advice might have been imparted to CEO Brett Berger as he began the journey in 1997?

More important, what can be learned from the GMI story that would offer real value to you if your company were suddenly thrust into rapid organizational change—or if you were thrust into a role like Brett Berger's? Are large I/T-based strategic transformations simply unmanageable? Or might there exist some form of procedure manual and management checklist of issues to address to guide one on such a journey? We believe that such a guide does exist, and our goal in this book is to explain it.

This chapter provides a framework for managing I/T investment opportunities and for overcoming the types of obstacles that were described in Chapter One. The framework offers a language with which to clarify the need for, nature of, and goals assigned to strategic I/T investments. It also provides a road map and a set of steps for achieving the purpose of those investments.

Our framework consists of two models that have evolved out of previous work done with Accenture. The first, called the *Business Architecture Model,* describes five dimensions in which a business and its operations might change as a result of strategic choices. This holistic view of organizational change positions a proposed I/T investment within the broader picture of a company's environment, strategy, processes, infrastructures, and performance objectives. To be successful, I/T investments need to be understood and planned within this wider context. The second model, called the *Journey Management Model,* lays out key activities that occur over time as a company moves from one business architecture to another. This strategic transition occurs in three phases: formulation, preparation, and implementation. Both models are useful in all three phases.

Initially, during strategy formulation, the models can help to gather and organize facts into a meaningful structure. They can guide the recognition of pathological patterns in those facts, and aid in the diagnosis of problem symptoms when they exist. Second, during preparation, the models become a form of pilot's checklist that assures consideration of the support required from people, processes, and technology. Finally, during implementation, the models provide a unifying reference point for the key tasks of building, testing, and deploying the new business processes that are enabled by the I/T investment.

■ The Business Architecture Model

The Business Architecture Model introduced here summarizes a set of commonly understood business concepts and establishes a vocabulary that we will use later as we discuss difficulties encountered during a business transformation. The model describes an ongoing business at a point in time in terms of five elements: strategic context, business strategy, performance, business processes, and infrastructure. Figure 2.1 illustrates that within a strategic context a selected business strategy will achieve targeted performance goals through the operation of business processes that are supported by organization and process infrastructure. These five elements interact. The heightened performance goals of a new business strategy often give rise to a search for improved business processes. New business processes in turn may require supporting infrastructure investments. And strategic context, finally, may determine the degree of process and infrastructure change that is feasible.

A business transformation is destined to fail if it focuses attention or investments on a single architecture element (such as new process infrastructure) while ignoring influences from and dependencies upon the others. Synergies and interdependencies among these architectural elements give strategic change its unique character and also make the process complex to manage.

Your Analysis

Before we elaborate on the elements of business architecture below, consider the following questions. In your experience,

1. What elements of strategic context can act to either enable or inhibit a business strategy?
2. What are characteristics of a sound business strategy and what essential questions must that strategy answer for a firm?

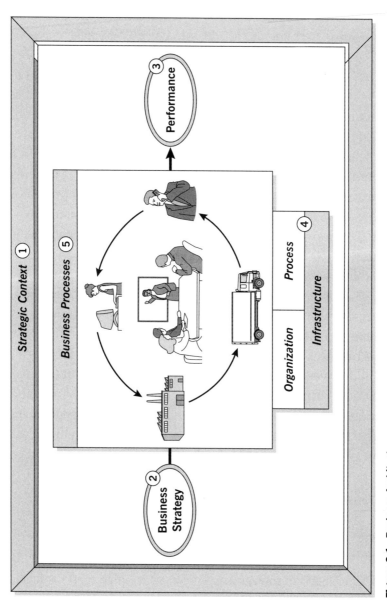

Figure 2.1. Business Architecture.

3. What role do measures of performance play in the creation or execution of a strategy?
4. How might a firm's business processes relate to changes in its business strategy?
5. What infrastructures exist within a firm and how might investments in them create strategic value?

Elements of a Business Architecture

As outlined in Figure 2.1, the business architecture of a firm consists of five interconnected elements: strategic context, business strategy, performance, business processes, and infrastructure. It's useful to look more closely at each one.

Strategic Context

The *strategic context* of an enterprise consists of conditions and facts that are difficult or impossible for a company to change. The context includes both the culture of the company itself and the environmental realities in which the company operates. Changes in strategic context will often precipitate a change in business strategy; in addition, a specific context will limit what is possible in the nature and degree of strategic change.

The environmental reality within which a business strategy is executed includes the economic, regulatory, technological, and infrastructural limitations of the countries and locations in which the business operates. It also includes the cultural and societal norms of the people who live there, the needs of the markets that the business might serve, and the appetite and capabilities of the companies with which the business collaborates or competes. Changing these factors generally lies beyond the abilities of an individual company and, therefore, strategy must be adapted and attuned to these realities.

The company culture has two components: the underlying values and beliefs of employees, and the mores and rituals of the organization itself. Attempts to change core values and beliefs of employees are fraught with difficulty, and one might argue inappropriate for a business manager. And because a business strategy will fail if it is incompatible with basic values of those who implement it, strategy must be crafted with this constraint in mind.

Similarly, the mores and rituals of an enterprise cannot be changed quickly, and strategic initiatives that are inconsistent with them cannot be sustained. In the medium to long term, however, changes to an enterprise's core values and beliefs are possible and can be effected with redesign of its organizational structure, governance processes, performance systems, and competency set—as discussed later under the topic of organizational infrastructure. Nevertheless, such contextual changes require careful management and must precede the introduction of process changes that conflict with the existing context.

Business Strategy
A business strategy and its complementary measures of performance are essential to motivate, direct, and control a successful organizational change. To be effective, strategy must be clear and specific but also realistic. To this end, strategy must temper innovative thinking with a sound grasp of practical reality. It must strike a delicate balance between what is desirable and what is possible. It does this by combining ideas for new products and services with insights about the organization's strengths, skills, and capacity for change. The strategy formulation process produces a plan that can be successfully communicated, resourced, and implemented.

To establish a business strategy, a general manager must first provide the answer to the fundamental question: *Where and how will we compete?* More specifically,

- What business opportunities will our company pursue?
- Which customers and geographic markets will we target?

- Which products and services will we offer?
- How will we differentiate our products or services from those of our competitors?
- What must our company do better than any of our competitors in order to realize our goals?

With a statement of the company's strategic vision, the general manager then needs to guide the formulation of operating plans which will achieve that strategy. This poses a second fundamental question: *What actions must we take to pursue our strategy?*

- What business capabilities will we have when we achieve the vision?
- Which capabilities do we already have and which do we need to develop?
- What is the appropriate design of the new capabilities?
- Should we build these capabilities ourselves or acquire, outsource, or establish an alliance with a third party?
- How can we galvanize our people around a coherent plan of action to pursue the changes necessary for success?
- Who will be responsible for each of the activities and outcomes required to achieve our objectives?
- How will we measure progress on our journey, and how will we know when we have arrived at our destination?

The essence of the final question is: "What will guide us as we move from where we are to where we wish to go?" A plan for performance measurement provides the answer.

Performance
The performance component of the Business Architecture Model provides a basis for feedback to monitor the success of the business strategy in operation. It includes the entire spectrum of measurement from top-level organizational goals to individual incentive targets. Measures range from summary financial state-

ments collected quarterly for external review to detailed work cell data gathered in real time and displayed for immediate reaction. Performance is thus tracked at multiple levels with various measures at different times.

Performance measures change over time to reflect not only changes in overall strategy but also changes in mid-level initiatives and priorities. The appropriate performance measures change as the strategy changes and also as actual performance changes, as with revised stretch goals for an individual or organization.

Because people and organizations will perform as they are measured, it is essential that from the top to the bottom of the organization performance measures are aligned with the business strategy. It is likewise essential that the organization infrastructure (discussed next) align with both the strategy and the performance system. For example, if individuals are to be held accountable for key performance measures, they will need the resources and the authority to make the decisions necessary to achieve success. Alignment is a continuing concern as facts change and strategy shifts.

Infrastructure
A company's infrastructure takes two forms: organization infrastructure and process infrastructure. *Organization infrastructure* consists of the roles, relationships, authority, accountability, knowledge, and competencies upon which effective business processes depend. *Process infrastructure* consists of the physical plant, facilities, equipment, and systems required to move materials and information through and among those processes.

Organization infrastructure defines "the way things work around here." By specifying the nature of accepted and expected behaviors, it acts as an invisible hand to guide and coordinate individuals and their activities in pursuit of a business strategy. As illustrated in Figure 2.2, it consists of three elements: structure, governance, and competency.

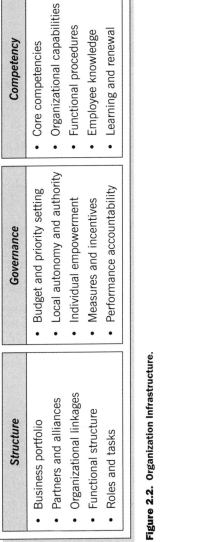

Structure	Governance	Competency
• Business portfolio	• Budget and priority setting	• Core competencies
• Partners and alliances	• Local autonomy and authority	• Organizational capabilities
• Organizational linkages	• Individual empowerment	• Functional procedures
• Functional structure	• Measures and incentives	• Employee knowledge
• Roles and tasks	• Performance accountability	• Learning and renewal

Figure 2.2. Organization Infrastructure.

Structure specifies individual and organizational roles and linkages. It includes the formal and informal relationships that exist among organizations and between individuals. It defines tasks and reporting relationships for these entities, and it establishes expectations for work products and levels of mutual support.

Governance establishes individual and organizational authority and accountability. It specifies the distribution of power within an organization and establishes procedures that will determine who gets to make decisions, what activities are given priority, what plans get funded, and what results are rewarded. Through budgets, targets, and incentives, governance guides the organization in day-to-day decision making.

Competency consists of the knowledge, skills, and capabilities of individuals and organizations within an enterprise. Changes in business processes imply changes in requisite competencies. The collection of competencies needed by a company therefore evolves over time with changes in business strategy. Thus the need for capability assessment and renewal is ongoing.

During strategic change, much attention is focused on frontline workers and their ability to perform new tasks. Much less energy is directed at the definition and development of the skill set required by middle and senior management to organize and direct such change in the first place. The ability to manage an organizational transformation remains a difficult competency to develop. This book is designed to support that need.

Process infrastructure defines "how things move around and through the enterprise." As illustrated in Figure 2.3, it has two components: information technology and production technology.

Information technology (I/T) infrastructure includes the hardware, software, data, and network components and architecture that underlie the creation and exchange of information with

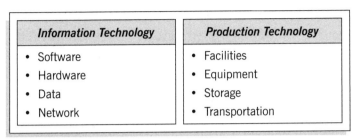

Information Technology	Production Technology
• Software	• Facilities
• Hardware	• Equipment
• Data	• Storage
• Network	• Transportation

Figure 2.3. Process Infrastructure.

which the business processes operate. The I/T architecture specifies the standards for and the locations of the firm's I/T components. Specifically, it determines what types of hardware and software may be employed; where exactly the people, equipment, data, and facilities will be located; how much application, data, and procedures compatibility will exist among locations; and how locations will be connected, coordinated, and controlled. The infrastructure reflects structure and governance choices that have been made regarding the degree of centralization of I/T activities and the reliance on outsourcing and alliances to achieve required competencies. The infrastructure acts to assure that I/T services are available, reliable, scalable, flexible, connectable, effective, and efficient.

Production technology infrastructure includes the facilities, equipment, storage, and transportation that move components and products around and through the enterprise. Inherent in the design of this infrastructure are basic investment trade-offs among inventory, capacity, customer service, and information technology. To design this infrastructure appropriately, a general manager must understand not only how products and services must be presented to the marketplace, but also how key product components can be acquired with speed, reliability, and quality while consuming minimal resources.

Essential for the success of a business strategy is a careful assessment of required infrastructure. Thus it is critical during strategy formulation to explicitly define each organization and process infrastructure component needed to shape and enable the planned business capabilities. Only in this context can infrastructure investments be adequately justified. And when needs are not defined, the yield from these investments will be predictably disappointing.

Business Processes

As the final element of business architecture, a corporation's business processes will work together to operationalize its business strategy. Figure 2.4 identifies three core processes (built on five functional systems) that are vital to the formulation and ex-

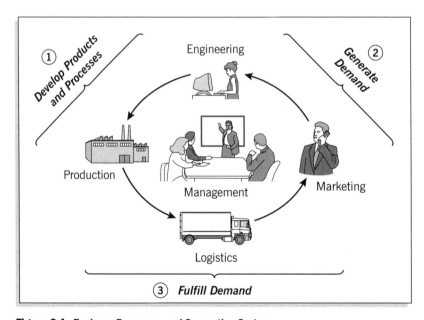

Figure 2.4. Business Processes and Supporting Systems.

ecution of any business strategy: product and process development, demand generation, and demand fulfillment.

Develop products and processes. This is achieved through a rapid and effective design and engineering capability linked to a flexible production capacity.

Generate demand. This is achieved through effective market intelligence and the responsive reengineering of processes, products, and services.

Fulfill demand. This is achieved through the efficient production of products and services supported by a reliable logistics system that responds quickly to customer requirements.

Processes, Infrastructure, and I/T Investment

The operations of the three business processes depend on five functional systems: production, logistics, marketing, engineering, and management. And the operation of these systems in turn depends on a firm's infrastructure. Thus I/T infrastructure investments create strategic value indirectly by improving the performance of the functional systems and in turn the business processes on which a firm's strategy is based.

Today, I/T investment is a powerful lever to enable and drive new business strategy. I/T infrastructure investment can lower the operating costs and improve the capabilities of functional systems and business processes, and thus such investment is justified because of its linkage to the business strategy that it supports. But conversely, I/T infrastructure investments may fail because of this linkage. Strategic changes to business processes can disrupt established professional relationships and may have negative effects on people's lives. To block an unwanted strategic initiative, an opponent might choose simply to thwart implementation of an enabling I/T investment. The journey management model that follows provides assistance in reducing this risk.

Your Analysis

Before we proceed to the journey model, consider these questions. In your experience,

1. What is the role of a firm's marketing system as it interfaces with its customers? How does I/T act to support this interface?
2. How does the engineering system work to maintain the quality of the products and business processes of a firm? How does I/T act to support these activities?
3. How does the production system operate to keep the marketing promises of a firm while producing products in a fast and efficient manner? How does I/T act to support production?
4. How does the logistics system operate to move materials to and through the firm in support of production and distribution? How might I/T support logistics?
5. What are the activities of the management system that assure the effective operation of the firm in pursuit of its business strategy? How does I/T change the nature of data that is available to accomplish these activities?

■ The Journey Management Model

A strategic transformation is difficult to accomplish even when managed well, and it is impossible when managed poorly. By "managed well" we mean that the change is directed by an acknowledged leader, guided by a well-defined process, and focused on clear objectives. To be successful the leader must first establish the purpose of the change and the steps required to accomplish it, and then assure that sufficient time and resources are allocated for the execution of those steps.

The model of Journey Management structures the process of strategic change by identifying the sequence in which key activities must occur over time as an organization proceeds through a strategic transformation. The model supports strategy execution by addressing the following human resource concerns:

- How do we enable the executives of a firm to both recognize the need for strategic redirection and to develop a workable plan for addressing that need?
- How do we prepare managers and workers to accept and support a strategic plan once it is developed?
- How do we help these individuals to visualize the operation of a new business organization and their role in it?
- How do we get them to accept responsibility for the design of the infrastructure that will support the changed operations?
- How do we properly prepare them for and involve them in the implementation and operation of those systems?
- How do we guarantee that they have the knowledge and skills to be successful in their new positions?
- How do we assure that the new procedures are accepted and applied effectively by those who must use and maintain them over time?
- How do we make certain that all of this is successfully accomplished over a multiyear period in the face of changing organizational capabilities, needs, and priorities?

Effective answers to these questions emerge naturally from the model described here. As illustrated by Figure 2.5, a change journey progresses from left to right through six stages: business diagnosis, strategy definition, capability analysis, detailed design, build and test, and capability deployment. These stages pair up into the three journey phases that we call formulation, preparation, and implementation. As a journey progresses, its work divides first into multiple programs during strategy definition and then further into multiple projects during detailed design. Each program is designed to deliver one or more new business capabilities and to resolve conflicts among related

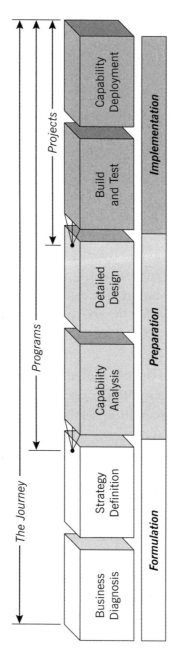

Figure 2.5. The Journey of Organizational Change.

projects that affect common business functions, facilities, equipment, schedules, or people.

Phase 1. Formulation

Formulation is the journey phase in which facts and assumptions are collected and used to establish the need for strategic change and the objectives of the journey. This phase also prescribes actions to achieve those objectives. Formulation is accomplished in two stages: business diagnosis and strategy definition.

Business Diagnosis

Business diagnosis develops an assessment of the firm's strategic context and creates an awareness of the facts that motivate change. This stage builds an understanding of the firm's competitive environment and strategic alternatives.

When exploring the competitive environment, it is useful to ask: What are the facts that prompt us to change? What are the external environment and market dynamics of our organization? How do the organization's financial condition, market position, and operating performance compare to those of its peers and competitors? Why would we choose to change what we are currently doing; what benefits are likely to be achieved? What are the existing market requirements, competitive threats, and regulatory obligations? Is there widespread acknowledgment of the need for change?

Based on answers to such questions, the next step is to examine both the status quo and strategic alternatives: What is our current business strategy and how well is it working? What are our comparative strengths and vulnerabilities? What strategic alternatives might the company pursue? What aspects of company culture or business environment constrain the alternatives?

What are our current capabilities and thus what choices for change are feasible for our organization at this time? What strategic actions are desirable—and which ones are clearly necessary? What degree of process change is necessary and what is possible? What gaps are there in organizational capability and infrastructure?

Strategy Definition
Strategy definition applies the knowledge gained during business diagnosis to craft the business vision that will drive the strategic journey. This vision consists of a business strategy, its performance objectives, an operating plan to achieve those objectives, and a business case that justifies the effort.

The *business strategy* provides a clear statement of what an organization intends to become, what businesses it chooses to be in, what purpose it seeks to achieve, and how it intends to serve its markets to build sustainable competitive advantage and create value. This direction is critical to focus the collective energy and efforts of the change journey. Subsequent design and implementation efforts must be closely aligned with this strategy to enable the firm to achieve its goals.

The *performance objectives* scope the nature and degree of improvement to which the firm aspires. They define the customer service, financial, and operational performance targets for the new business processes and provide the basis for measuring success during and after the implementation phase.

The *operating plan* looks at the internal approaches for key processes, capabilities, or systems that will best achieve the firm's strategic vision. The plan is the conceptual design of the operating model. It forces disciplined, up-front thinking about how the new business capabilities will be developed. First, overall business objectives and performance targets are established. Then plausible operating alternatives are evaluated and the best is determined. For the selected alternative, an overall operating model is created and its underlying capabilities are identified.

The *business case* provides a rationale for change and sets targets for the new organization. It creates a practical and integrated implementation plan and spells out how the new business capabilities will be phased into the organization. Performance targets are established for each capability, and milestones are identified at which specific levels of performance and value will be achieved. Journey costs and business benefits are estimated. The business case thus provides points of reference from which the work of strategy implementation can be focused on delivering value.

The preliminary business architecture defined by these four strategic elements is a living document that takes on more detail during the formulation phase and evolves continually as the journey progresses. The architecture at any moment provides management with a powerful vehicle for building and sustaining commitment to change. From it, people within the organization—and especially the people who will be doing the work—will know where the organization is heading, how it is going to get there, and how they are expected to contribute.

Phase 2. Preparation

Preparation is the middle journey phase, the one that ensures the infrastructures, resources, and accountabilities needed for success. A plan for realizing the business capabilities of each journey program spells out, in practical terms, how the organization will make the transition from its current state to the desired future. It describes how and when individual projects will be undertaken, how new business capabilities will be released into the organization, what resources will be required, and what value will be realized at interim points along the way. It proceeds through two activities: capability analysis and detailed design.

Capability Analysis
Capability analysis aligns organization and process infrastructures with the operating plan. What lack of organization structure, governance procedures, and competencies will inhibit implementation of the new business processes? What new capacities will be required for the exchange of information and the movement of material through the new organization? What changes or enhancements in human resources are required to support the business process changes?

Detailed Design
Detailed design divides the work required into manageable projects and clusters these logically into programs based on shared resources or affected functions. Prior estimates of the timing and magnitude of costs and benefits are made more precise at this point. Have planned programs been broken into projects that achieve measurable goals? What are the best grouping, sequence, and pace for the execution of these projects? What people, facilities, equipment, time, capital, and operating expense will be needed to execute each program? Who and what will be made available at what specific time? Is the implementation schedule feasible and is it reasonably certain that the resources will exist and that they will be made available on a sustained basis?

If the journey is to succeed, accountability for the achievement of milestones and performance goals must be assigned to capable management. What are the required roles and responsibilities that must be assigned to accomplish the business case? What is it that each participant in the transition will be required to do both during the journey and afterward, and is it reasonable to expect that those individuals will be able and motivated to do what is necessary? Is the business case viable and sufficiently detailed, and is there an associated performance model that defines the expected improvement of what by whom and by when?

Phase 3. Implementation

Implementation is the final journey phase. Here the program plans and resources are brought together to achieve planned business capabilities through two activities: build and test, and capability deployment.

Build and Test
Build and test activities execute the plans designed during preparation. This stage of the journey builds, assembles, and tests each element of new technology, business process, and human performance that underlies a new business capability. Its product is a pilot demonstration of how the capability achieves its planned objectives. The work of this stage is to build the capability and test it at the levels of individual components and the complete assembly. These tests assure that the capability meets the design requirements and achieves planned performance. It also validates that the capability fits within the overall infrastructure and integrates with other capabilities.

Capability Deployment
Capability deployment introduces the new capability into targeted operating units. This stage can be a long and complex logistical exercise involving a large number of interrelated activities. New facilities may need to be outfitted, a new technology or new operating procedures may need to be implemented. Also people may need to accept and adapt to new ways of working, learn new skills, and strive for new levels of performance. Integral to successful deployment are new management processes to verify and sustain the planned improvements in business performance once a new business capability is deployed.

In general, the deployment stage tailors the new business capability and the way that it is rolled out according to local operation and market conditions. Once the new capability is in place, legacy processes are removed to formally signal the transition to the new capability. The operation of the capability is stabilized before passing management responsibility to line personnel. And appropriate management metrics, service level agreements, and operating level agreements are activated to realize the business performance model.

Managing the Phases of the Journey

Figure 2.6 summarizes the key activities performed in each journey phase as it proceeds over time. A journey of long duration can go disastrously off course when the facts of the situation change

Formulation
- Collect facts that motivate the need for change; create organizational readiness.
- Identify comparative benchmarks; establish performance objectives and gaps in capability.
- Consider strategic alternatives; assure interorganizational involvement.
- Determine strategic objectives and operating strategy; build and share a business case for change.

Preparation
- Specify functional capability and infrastructure requirements; prioritize journey tasks.
- Appropriate people, authority and resources; schedule implementation of tasks.
- Establish targets and timing; personalize performance measures.
- Clarify and adapt strategy and objectives as required.

Implementation
- Acquire skills and build prerequisite infrastructure; assure feedback and control.
- Build, test, and deploy capability releases; adjust to local needs and conditions.
- Exercise new capabilities; stabilize work practices, activate performance models.
- Adjust budgeted resources and schedule as required.

Project Management Program Management Journey Management

Figure 2.6. Key Activities in Each Journey Phase.

but resources, schedule, and scope of programs are not adjusted in an appropriate and timely fashion. Therefore, three overlapping management processes (at the right in Figure 2.6) act to monitor and direct journey activities. Journey management, program management, and project management each initially guides the planning activity of its associated phase and then monitors progress against the plan to assure design integrity as conditions, facts, and assumptions change over time. This feedback affords opportunities to adjust goals, resources, and schedules during program implementation as events, experience, and insights dictate. A key finding of our research is that the primary cause of the implementation problems that occur during a journey of strategic change is the failure to recognize and appropriately respond to shifts in strategic context. Vigilance for signs of such context shifts and willingness to adapt plans quickly are critical to maintaining management control over a strategic journey. Three parallel activities are needed to keep the journey on track: journey management, program management, and project management.

Journey Management

Journey management focuses on delivering success through the attainment of planned business results. It is driven by the organization's senior leadership and it works by ensuring that the right programs and projects are defined and that the organization is able and motivated to take advantage of the resulting capabilities as they are delivered. Journey management requires that planned changes are aligned with strategic priorities and have a clear business case. It ensures that sponsor and stakeholder expectations are clearly articulated, monitored, and managed throughout the change journey and that those charged to lead the change are equipped with the skills and capacity needed to be effective. It tracks the progress of the change initiative—monitoring factors such as ongoing ownership and commitment, benefits realization, program progress, and changes in context—so that adjustments to the course of action can be made as necessary.

Program Management

Program management directs multiple projects to deliver one or more planned business capabilities by applying appropriate disciplines, tools, and techniques to organize and coordinate the work. It assures a continuous cycle of planning the work, setting priorities, assigning responsibilities, and determining timetables. Program management also coordinates the dependencies between projects, assesses and controls overall program risks, and reports on the progress. It is at this level that the delivery of planned business capabilities is achieved.

Project Management

Project management focuses on producing specific deliverables, such as process infrastructure, information system applications, and reengineered business processes. With a concern for successful delivery it brings discipline and predictability to the project. Once given a clearly defined set of tasks with specific and measurable outcomes, it carefully manages project scope, schedule, risk, and effort quality. It provides the continuous direction needed to plan and manage project tasks in a cost-effective manner. Thirty years ago the management of I/T-based projects was a challenge, but today the field has matured with proven methodologies that assure the reliable delivery of I/T projects once they have been clearly specified and allocated sufficient resources.

The Critical Role of Recurring Transitional Assessments

A key task of management is the continuous monitoring of journey activities to assess whether facts or conditions have changed sufficiently to warrant an adaptation of current plans. Such assessments verify not only the appropriateness of current plans, but also the organization's current readiness to move forward on the journey in the light of new circumstances.

Transitions that might merit an assessment vary. It could be an external event (a new customer requirement), a shift in the internal environment (a redefinition of business priorities), a project event (an unexpected delay), the passage of time (a monthly review), or a specific point in the journey (the start or end of an activity). Transitional assessments raise the basic question, Where are we right now? This question leads to others: Do the assumptions that guide us still hold; do our plans still make sense? Are our resources adequate; is our schedule achievable? What do we know now that we did not know previously that might make a difference in our projects, programs, or journey?

The three journey phases each start with a scheduled moment for reassessment. Here a review of organization readiness to proceed with the journey is both vital and natural and therefore should be mandatory. But, in addition, more frequent periodic reviews (say monthly) of journey progress are important during Phases 1 and 2. During Phase 3, weekly reviews are absolutely essential.

■ Applying the Models

The next four chapters will apply the Business Architecture and Journey Management models to describe the events of the GMI case and to diagnose how, when, and why problems arose during strategy implementation. Although Figure 2.5 depicts sharp boundaries between the stages and phases of the journey, in fact these boundaries are blurry. Some journey activities blend into one another, while others can occur in parallel. In-depth study of the GMI case will reveal, for example, that infrastructure implementation could and did take place in parallel with preparations to improve global manufacturing processes. Nonetheless, there remains a basic precedence for successful organizational change—formulate, prepare, and implement. Effective action can never get ahead of its purpose and preparation.

SUMMARY

In summary, our framework consists of two models. First, the *Business Architecture Model* identifies five dimensions in which a business and its operations might change as a result of strategic choices. The model provides a snapshot of an ongoing business in terms of five elements: strategic context, business strategy, performance, business processes, and infrastructure. It observes that within a strategic context a selected business strategy achieves its targeted performance goals through the operation of business processes that are supported by organization and process infrastructure.

Second, the *Journey Management Model* lays out key activities in three phases that occur over time as a company moves from one business architecture to another. Phase 1 formulates a preliminary business architecture. Phase 2 provides additional details for this architecture and makes preparations for required business process changes. And Phase 3 implements these process changes and ensures that the planned benefits are harvested.

Questions for Consideration

1. This model of plan-prepare-implement is simple to describe. If it has true value, what could explain why firms so rarely adhere to it?
2. How important do you believe are the management processes that monitor and adapt plans during a journey of long duration? Why?
3. Have you had experiences in which a large development program attained so much momentum during its implementation that it was difficult to control? What was the cause, and what might be a cure?

3

Formulating Strategy

C hapter Two described two business models that are useful in directing complex change within organizations and
in analyzing historical cases of such change. Recall that
the Business Architecture Model defines the key elements of
business that are affected by a strategic change, and that the
Journey Management Model structures, identifies, and appropriately sequences the key activities required to accomplish such
change. This chapter will begin to use those models to study the
case of Global Manufacturing Incorporated (GMI), a fictionalized composite of a large corporation that began to invest heavily in I/T-related changes beginning in 1997. We will follow the
case from beginning to end, using the models to divide it into

stages and to guide us through a series of analytic questions. Our goal is to see what kinds of problems arose for GMI and to judge how effectively the company dealt with them. Before giving our own analysis of events, step-by-step along the way we will ask you to perform your own analysis.

In this chapter, we'll cover the stages of Business Diagnosis and Strategy Definition that together constitute Phase 1 of the Journey Management Model. Chapters Four, Five, and Six will continue our analysis and by the end of Chapter Six, you'll fully appreciate the value of the models in the difficult process of becoming an information-enabled company.

As you are likely to know from experience, large-scale corporate change is multifaceted. And thus only a relatively intricate case study can do a discussion of it justice. You will see that the GMI case is realistically complex. It represents the combined experience of ten corporations that we studied in detail as they undertook changes in business processes led by information technology, plus input from scores of companies that we have worked with over the past thirty years. Working slowly through the case, we'll explore its complexity by uncovering key steps and decisions made over a six-year period and addressing the challenges they posed.

GMI did many things well, but it left a few critical events unmanaged. Despite competent leadership, high aspirations, strong commitment, a reasonable plan, and a specific purpose, under pressure of unplanned events it drifted off course. One great value of our models is that they help identify dimensions and moments when developing problems can be recognized and resolved before they have an opportunity to compromise later success.

Our thesis is that if the leadership of GMI had appropriately applied the Journey Management Model, the chances of a successful conclusion to their change process would have been substantially improved. With it they would have been better able to anticipate and deal with inevitable shifts in strategic context and business priorities. The Business Architecture Model would have been useful in providing a vocabulary with which to describe events as they unfolded and in discussing the actions needed to deal with unanticipated problems. It would have, for example, helped to identify infrastructure components in which investments were needed but overlooked.

■ GMI Prior to 1997

GMI grew out of an industrial forging company that was founded in 1922 and diversified in the 1940s. It grew in multinational status during the 1970s and adopted the name Global Manufacturing Incorporated in 1976. For twenty years thereafter, GMI operated as a tight ship—management consciously maintained a lean corporate overhead structure while investing capital in new plant and equipment only when presented with a clear business case and a payback period of three years or less. The performance of the business unit presidents was measured on return-on-net-assets (RONA). They too, therefore, watched both overhead costs and asset deployment quite closely. For some time, a source of some pride within the company was the ability to hold the corporate I/T budget below 1.5 percent of revenues while the average for the industry was running at a little over 2.9 percent. Possibly due to this lack of technology investment, however, other administrative and operating expenses were noticeably higher than industry averages.

Over decades of marketplace success, GMI grew complacent and bureaucratic. By 1996 it was facing hard economic times and some tough strategic choices. It was encountering increasingly aggressive foreign competition, and its financial performance had turned dramatically downward. The company was suffering from high production costs and falling revenues, driven both from the outside by changing customer needs and aggressive competition and from the inside by growing bureaucracy and loss of competency.

In an effort to counter the profit downturn, in 1996 GMI's management hastily launched a two-year recovery program called "Operational Excellence." This program aimed at improving profitability in product sales and service by reducing inventories, delays, overhead, and scrap. Operational Excellence was bottom-up reengineering modeled after the "Work-Out" initiative developed at General Electric, whose success had been widely reported in the business press. The hope at GMI was to enlist the workforce to identify sources of inefficiency and quality failures so that these problems could be solved. A group of university faculty was hired to deliver classes on reengineering, Six-Sigma quality, and process mapping. The rallying cry for the GMI program became "Doing Better By Working Smarter."

Operational Excellence focused almost exclusively on cost reduction activities and did little to address the equally important problem of revenue deterioration. Thus it was met with immediate skepticism and suspicion by GMI's unions. Workers feared that the program's real aim was not to improve customer satisfaction but to eliminate jobs. Operational Excellence relied for success on a pair of initiatives called "Employee Involvement" and "Total Quality Management." Both initiatives collapsed—taking Operational Excellence down with them—when employees learned that management had budgeted for a 1997 corporate restructuring that would eliminate 16 percent of the workforce. Factory operations immediately began to suffer from quality problems, lost production, and missed shipments.

With the collapse of Operational Excellence, the board of directors sought a new beginning for the GMI recovery. Brett Berger, the charismatic and hard-charging SVP of marketing within the Industrial division, was promoted to CEO. Realizing that his challenge was to redefine GMI's strategic direction and having no personal experience as a leader of strategic change, he immediately sought help.

Berger engaged an executive search firm to locate a senior executive with substantial experience in leading transformational change in large manufacturing corporations. Aware that many strategic changes had been going well at General Electric, Berger directed the search firm's attention toward GE. Along with candidates from other companies, the search firm identified Harry Linker, a divisional CFO in GE, as a person who could lead the transformation at GMI. The search firm believed that Linker could not only guide Berger in the formation of a new strategy but also spearhead the change effort for him.

Several meetings, both formal and informal, took place between the two men in the fall of 1996, during which they discussed the challenges before GMI and the failure of the Operational Excellence program. From his experience at GE, Linker understood immediately that GMI had tried to move forward with its program of change too quickly and without a holistic strategy. He put it this way:

"There are some natural progressions in organizational change that need to be followed carefully—first you put on your pants, *then* you put on your shoes. I have found that employees will adjust to any reasonable set of changes, but they need to be properly prepared for them. They want to be told why; they should understand how; they need to be properly equipped; and they must believe in the integrity of their leadership and the soundness of their strategy.

"To this end, we as general managers have an obligation to plan our change programs carefully and then to communicate them clearly, widely, frequently, and consistently. We need to link our performance measurement systems to the planned changes and connect both to our strategic objectives; we must see to it that needed skills are developed in our people, and we must assure that required organizational and technical infrastructures are available when needed."

The chemistry between the two men felt right to Berger. He came to believe that Linker was not only a man who could shake things up at GMI but also one who could catalyze and lead the company forward on the path where Operational Excellence had failed. He presented Harry Linker the challenge of leading the development of a new strategic plan for GMI and offered him the position of Chief Financial Officer. With assurances from Berger that he understood the dimensions and magnitude of the journey before them, and after frank discussions with key members of GMI's board of directors, Linker accepted the offer. He came on board in January 1997.

Your Analysis

1. Is this a familiar pattern of difficulties for companies in the 1990s? What was wrong with the "Operational Excellence" recovery program as executed?
2. As Linker assessed the situation at GMI, what evidence suggested that the company was ready to face the difficult challenges of a strategic transformation? What minimum set of prerequisites is necessary at this point in time?

What Went Wrong with the GMI Recovery Program

GMI's basic problem of shifting market requirements, emerging technology capabilities, and falling profit margins is all too familiar to many traditional manufacturing companies. It's no surprise that the Operational Excellence program failed to solve GMI's problems. After all, industry studies report that only 10 percent of all reengineering efforts conclude with what is labeled success. In the case of GMI, we believe that the program failed because it lacked a holistic business strategy. It focused too heavily on cost reduction and neglected to address the equally important issues of declining revenues and emerging technologies.

Process reengineering alone could not have produced the transformational changes needed to save GMI. The reengineering program began with the simplistic argument, "If we improve our current performance by working smarter at what we do, then we will sharpen our execution and thereby surpass our competition at the current game." But that argument fails if the current game has been fundamentally altered by new rules, as it had for GMI with the advent of e-business (which was changing the nature of business relationships) and the arrival of aggressive foreign competitors who were drawing from a dramatically less expensive labor pool. In this situation, the company needed a new organization, new equipment, new skills, new players, new plays, and, most important, a new business strategy.

As for what the reengineering program was trying to do, simple directives like "do better by working smarter" will leave employees confused when, for example, choices collide between improvements in plant utilization, inventory investment, and customer service. This bottom-up plan lacked a strategic focus. Trade-offs will always exist between competing performance measures, and good trade-off choices can only be judged in the context of a specific business strategy. It was only natural that the workforce withdrew its support from a program whose main thrust was perceived as personnel reduction. Basically, Operational Excellence was a hopeless attempt to bandage a growing cancer.

An Initial Transitional Assessment

Linker did not leap blindly into the opportunity presented to him at GMI. As he was being interviewed by Berger and the board for the position of CFO, he was interviewing them as well to assess whether they were prepared to support a true strategic transformation at GMI. He understood from experience that at the outset of a journey of strategic change, three questions of organizational readiness were key to eventual success. These questions relate to management, sponsors, and the change team:

- Is there an executive management consensus around the need for strategic change?
- Are influential sponsors for the change program visible and supportive?
- Has a cross-functional change team been committed to the program, and does this team have the experience, skills, and organizational credibility needed for success?

On the basis of his interviews Linker believed that the first two prerequisites were in place and that the third could be quickly established. With a clear mandate for change from the board and visible support from Brett Berger, Linker knew that he would be able to gather a blue-ribbon task force from across the organization to execute the process of strategy formulation. And to complement the business knowledge of this team, he could go outside the company as necessary for the technical skills needed to assess GMI's infrastructures. Believing that these three prerequisites for success were present, Linker accepted the GMI challenge and prepared to launch the process that would create a new strategic direction for the company.

■ Phase 1 (Part 1) Formulation: Business Diagnosis

With GMI as with any company, the first step is to diagnose the current state of the business and its needs going forward. For this Business Diagnosis four sets of questions need to be answered:

- What is the firm's current strategy for value creation and how well is it working? How do the firm's market position, operating performance, and financial condition compare to those of peers and competitors?
- What external environment and market dynamics are affecting the organization and its strategy? What market demands, competitive pressures, and regulatory requirements create pressure for change?
- Is there sufficient documentation of facts for a credible analysis and realistic assessment? Is there a common understanding of these facts and widespread acceptance of the implied need for change?
- What key strategic alternatives might the organization choose to pursue? What dimensions of company culture or competency can be leveraged moving forward? What aspects of company culture or business environment constrain alternatives? What strategic actions are desirable and which are clearly necessary?

Initial Moves (January 1997–May 1997)

Harry Linker joined GMI as CFO in January 1997 with a mandate to administer the development of a new strategic plan. Although he did not think of his task in the language of our Journey Management Model, he was about to lead GMI through what we would call the Business Diagnosis stage of Phase 1 with a significant effort aimed at redesigning the firm's Business Architecture.

GMI was composed of two divisions (Automotive and Industrial) plus a central support staff, as illustrated in Figure 3.1. With guidance and support from CEO Brett Berger, Linker soon gathered a cross-functional transition team of eight high-potential managers from multiple functions within both divisions. Their task was to propose a new strategic direction for

Global Manufacturing Incorporated

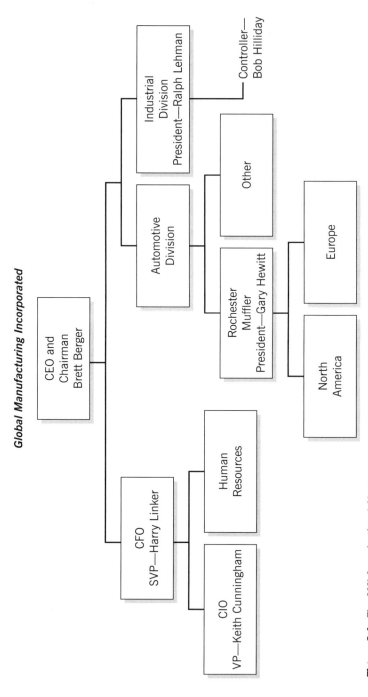

Figure 3.1. The GMI Organizational Chart.

GMI. To complement the strong business knowledge of this team, the technical skills needed to assess GMI's infrastructures would be acquired from outside the company as necessary.

For three months, Linker and his team traveled throughout the corporation taking the pulse of the operating divisions, developing an understanding of the business challenges that confronted them, and sizing up the quality of both their operations and their leadership. Strong pressures for change were documented by the team, as summarized in Figure 3.2. These pressures arose from both emerging customer requirements and an evolving business environment.

A clear organizational problem immediately documented by Linker's team was that the business units had overlapping customers, suppliers, distribution channels, and manufacturing technologies, but no one was coordinating the strategies of different units to take advantage of this scale. Even across operating locations in the same business unit there were uncoordinated purchase contracts, duplicate sales calls, manual consolidation of customer invoices, and replication of R&D activities. Benchmark comparisons with other companies in the industry revealed that business unit overhead was bloated, product development slow, product quality spotty, delivery unreliable, and inventories high.

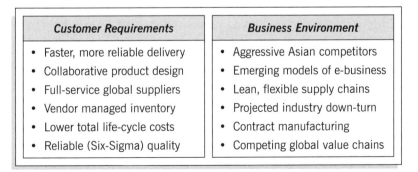

Customer Requirements	Business Environment
• Faster, more reliable delivery	• Aggressive Asian competitors
• Collaborative product design	• Emerging models of e-business
• Full-service global suppliers	• Lean, flexible supply chains
• Vendor managed inventory	• Projected industry down-turn
• Lower total life-cycle costs	• Contract manufacturing
• Reliable (Six-Sigma) quality	• Competing global value chains

Figure 3.2. Pressures for Change at GMI.

It was during this assessment that the combined business experience and cross-functional character of the task force members paid dividends. Because they were credible and trusted, the task force quickly identified evidence of strategic deficiencies. Obvious examples were compiled, categorized, and grouped according to GMI's core business processes of Demand Generation, Demand Fulfillment, and Product and Process Innovation, as shown in Figure 3.3. These findings were verified by team members with functional peers and during one-on-one presentations to key managers throughout the company. They were also shared with Brett Berger and the board during their regular updates on the progress of the task force.

Linker could trace many of these performance shortcomings in large part to GMI's use of outmoded operating practices. For example, manufacturing operations relied completely on a thirty-year-old production scheduling philosophy called materials requirements planning (MRP). When introduced in the late 1960s, MRP was an innovative procedure designed to carry out the complex activity of manufacturing planning by taking advantage of the calculating power of the era's "modern" computers. Those early MRP systems helped order planners schedule production and determine quantities of parts needed to meet a forecast for product shipments. In concept, an MRP system used procedures for bill-of-materials explosion, inventory netting, and back scheduling to determine when to place orders and then when to release work to production so that finished products would arrive "just in time" to satisfy an anticipated customer demand stream.

MRP had been successful in its day. The application of MRP software to GMI's production scheduling in 1970 had significantly reduced order lead times as well as inventories of raw materials, work-in-process, and finished goods. However, as Linker was aware, by the 1990s MRP had been eclipsed in other companies by more effective production scheduling practices. Newer computer-based technologies enabled information-sharing

Demand Generation	Demand Fulfillment	Product and Process Innovation
• Multiple conflicting points of contact	• Old, inconsistent manufacturing practices	• Competitors ahead in many key areas
• Unreliable sales forecasts	• Large batch, long cycle production	• Slowest design cycle in our industries
• Inaccurate available-to-promise data	• Production costs exceeding standards	• Product and component proliferation
• Slow and unreliable delivery	• High rate of scrap and customer returns	• Little reuse of standard components
• Price concessions to hold share	• Excessive inventory and overtime expense	• No involvement of partners in design
• Loss of key customer accounts	• Low employee morale and high turnover	• Incompatible CAD software and data

Figure 3.3. Current Performance Problems at GMI.

among supply-chain partners, which allowed further improvements in service and productivity that GMI had not achieved. To Linker it was clear that the only way to restore GMI's competitiveness was to redefine its business strategy and modernize its business practices and supporting technologies.

As Linker deepened his understanding of the company's capabilities and weaknesses, he was formulating an agenda for change. He became aware of GMI's historical self-image as a tight ship with lean corporate overhead and three-year horizons for investment payback. However, he also saw that administrative and operating expenses actually exceeded industry averages. Linker soon came to believe that the company's ability to cut expenses in the future depended on the reengineering of current business operations to take advantage of the coordination and leverage opportunities offered by new information technologies.

On the basis of similar initiatives at GE, he had an appreciation of the nature, scope, and duration of the work that lay ahead for GMI. It was substantial. He estimated that the entire change effort would take seven to ten years to complete, and in April 1997 he began referring to the vision for change as GMI-2004.

Your Analysis

1. Look back at the four factual questions of Business Diagnosis listed at the beginning of this section. Does it appear that Linker and his team were effectively gathering information to address them?
2. To what extent is Linker envisioning the GMI-2004 journey in terms of employing new information technology or otherwise making the company more information-enabled?
3. Look back also at Linker's original assessment of management, sponsor, and team readiness for strategic change. Does it look like the change team has the support and commitment that the journey will require? Any indications that support might be lacking now or later from Berger or the board of directors?

Assessment of Linker's First Steps

When Harry Linker arrived on the scene in January 1997, he brought with him a mental model of organizational change built from prior experiences. He knew immediately what to do. Although it was his professional instinct that told Linker what was needed, his actions at this point conform well to our model of Journey Management.

Linker first guided his team through a fact-finding effort that traveled throughout GMI's business units. The effort documented the condition of the company's processes and infrastructure and familiarized the team with the company's culture. The team also looked outside the company. They collected information on competitors, customers, and suppliers across all the segments in which GMI was competing. The team searched for unmet customer needs, untapped GMI capabilities, and benchmark standards of company performance. It became obvious from interviews with managers from inside and outside the firm that there was an urgent need to reestablish the business strategy of GMI.

The Four Factual Questions
We believe that Linker and his team conducted an effective fact-finding effort regarding the company and its competitors, customers, and suppliers, and thereby addressed well the four questions of Business Diagnosis. For example, they identified clear pressures for change and evidence of inadequate performance of core business processes, as summarized in Figures 3.2 and 3.3. With credible evidence of the need for change, the challenge then was to draw forward the alternative strategic actions that would correct these deficiencies. To this end the task force summarized its findings in the form of an executive briefing, which it disseminated in informal settings with functional peers and divisional colleagues of team members; it was also shared in one-on-one meetings with key members of the GMI management

team. This verification of facts was a precursor to an extended management retreat to be held later. The next sections pause to take a look at the situation from the inside, discussing the way things looked to Linker and his associates at this point in the project's development.

How Does This Project Aim to Strengthen GMI's I/T Capabilities?
Linker can see that the I/T systems at GMI have suffered from years of neglect and that significant enhancement of these capabilities will be required to achieve a business turnaround at GMI. However, I/T was not the focus of the business diagnosis, nor would it be the focus of the strategy formulation stage of journey management. Linker understands that until executive management reaches consensus on a business strategy to pursue, he will not be able to get a handle on the changes required in GMI's core business processes and functional systems. How much to spend on what pieces of I/T infrastructure, and with what priority, will flow eventually from that analysis.

The nettlesome problem here is that of "the chicken and the egg." I/T investments must await business strategy, but business strategy depends (at least in part) on the I/T capabilities of the firm—what is the degree of process change that can realistically be supported?

First Moment for Reassessment:
Management, Sponsor, and Team Readiness
At this point, GMI has reached the first of the three major moments for reassessment that the Journey Management model requires. Even though he isn't working with knowledge of that model, Linker is in reasonably good shape here.

1. *Executive management consensus on the need for strategic change?* Linker proceeds at this point with a strong sense of executive management consensus around the need for some sort of strategic change. However, he knows he has work to do in

getting their support for any specific plan for change and particularly in sustaining that support over the duration of the extended journey that he anticipates.

2. *Visible support of influential sponsors?* Right now, Linker is enjoying a honeymoon period of visible support by Berger and the board of directors. The assignment of key high-potential employees as members of the change team, their regular meetings with Berger, and their regular progress reports to the board are widely known within GMI, and thus executive support is clearly visible throughout the company. Linker is surely confident that Berger and the board are behind them at this point, but he's also preparing to do much more to solidify their commitment. In particular, the idea of a protracted seven-year journey is something to which they are unaccustomed; selling it to them implies a need for journey segmentation, program milestones, and early and regular deliverables.

3. *Commitment of an experienced, skilled, and credible cross-functional change team?* Linker addressed this prerequisite immediately by enlisting Berger's help in picking the right people. He was careful to represent both divisions on the team and to include enough team members to allow broad representation of each functional area. Linker undoubtedly believes that the intensive process of diagnosis across the corporation has widened the view of team members and deepened their commitment. The three-month process has also allowed Linker to see his task force in action and confirm that these people are capable.

■ Phase 1 (Part 2) Formulation: Strategy Definition

By leveraging the facts documented during the business diagnosis process, Linker can now begin to define a vision of change and define a strategy to accomplish it. As noted in Chapter Two, the vision includes four basic elements:

- *Business strategy:* What does the organization intend to become? What markets will it serve, and how? What value will
  it create, and what sustainable competitive advantage can it
  achieve?
- *Performance targets:* What is the basis for measuring success?
  And thus what degree of improvement and change is needed?
  How extensive must it be?
- *Operating plan:* What specific changes are needed in key
  processes, capabilities, or systems to hit the performance targets? What is the overall operating model? What underlying
  business capabilities will be needed?
- *Business case:* What is the rationale for the journey in terms
  of future financial returns? Who is accountable for delivering these benefits, and by when?

Next Steps (May–June, 1997)

Having completed an effective business diagnosis, Linker and his
task force were credibly prepared to propose actions that would
improve GMI's strategic position. They could now formulate a
strategic vision of where GMI was to move, establish a business
case that would justify the required investments, and define performance targets that would measure journey success. The team
attacked this task by posing and answering six questions:

- What is the new business vision that motivates the strategic
  changes that are proposed?
- What customers, geographies, products, and services are included in the new strategy? What value proposition will differentiate the firm's product and services?
- What performance measurement plan has been developed
  to judge progress and to gauge and reward success? What
  business capabilities are required to achieve these targets
  and what capability or infrastructure gaps must therefore be
  addressed?

- How will technology and people combine with business processes in an operating plan to deliver the planned business capabilities?
- How will the process changes needed to achieve the operating plan be phased into the organization, and what milestones, checkpoints, and measures will guide the implementation?
- What is the business case that details and documents the planned costs and benefits and how and when will achievement of the business case be measured?

Linker understood that GMI could reasonably pursue any of several business strategies and therefore that his team could not arbitrarily select one and present it to the organization as a fait accompli. For a plan to succeed, GMI management would first have to understand and buy in to the plan, and then they would have to work together to achieve it. Nevertheless, to move this process along, Linker did construct a loosely connected collection of task force proposals as a straw man for discussion with management. He intended to build consensus around a course of action by involving management in the final design.

The first step was to sell the findings and ideas to GMI's executive management. This began in private during May 1997 as Linker's task force visited each member of the management team for a briefing on the findings and some preliminary recommendations.

The task force then made a presentation of their findings at a three-day management retreat in June, addressing Brett Berger and the top thirty members of his management team. The retreat was a series of briefings and workshops. It was there that Linker presented the straw man strategy for discussion by the entire group. The retreat was designed to frame the discussion of strategic plans around key issues that Linker knew were important to those at the meeting. His intent was to reformulate the proposals to some degree and then refine them into a final strategic plan.

Retreat Day 1

The first morning was spent reviewing and reacting to the data collected by the task force and to the conclusions reached during their assessment. Based mainly on evidence brought to them by the task force, participants were able to agree on the nature of operating problems currently affecting GMI's core business processes of Demand Generation, Demand Fulfillment, and Product and Process Innovation (again see Figure 3.3).

The afternoon then turned to a discussion of the need for change and basic principles that should guide the development of a strategy. What emerged from that session were two lists that would later drive discussion and debate during the strategy formulation process (Figure 3.4). The first was a set of *guiding principles* that the group felt would be key to the success of any GMI strategy. The second was a set of *key business drivers* that participants believed should be used to focus the design of the strategy's new operating plan.

By the end of the first day, participants agreed that the next day could be devoted to formulating a future vision for GMI that addressed the problems thus far revealed.

Guiding Principles	Key Business Drivers
• Understand customer value and cost	• Enable profitable revenue growth
• Align business systems and strategy	• Build customer loyalty
• Partner with key global suppliers	• Adopt value-based product pricing
• Achieve information and process transparency	• Improve lead time, quality, cost
• Simplify organizational processes	• Involve and empower workers
• Leverage strengths globally	• Eliminate variability and waste
• Respect the dignity of employees	• Simplify value-chain transactions
• Encourage continuous improvement	• Improve asset utilization

Figure 3.4. Guides During Strategy Development at GMI.

Retreat Day 2
With the group already agreed on process, the second day focused on a future vision for GMI. The discussion shifted to what the group believed the company would look like in ten years if the strategy that they were about to develop were successful. In describing their vision, participants studied again the three business processes they had examined on the first day. Within each process, they brainstormed desired operating characteristics and synthesized the results. Those results, along with a corporate mission statement that the group adopted, are shown in Figure 3.5.

The managers reached consensus about how to measure improvements for each operating characteristic, as well as the level of performance they expected. The purpose of these quantitative goals was to aid translation from qualitative descriptions of business capabilities into the specific operating actions and process capabilities that GMI would need to develop. These numbers would subsequently inform the business process designers as to the scale and scope of the process changes needed and the size of the investments required. Eventually the numbers would also form a basis for measuring process performance and program achievement during Phase 3, Implementation.

Retreat Day 3
On the final day, the discussion turned to an actual development plan: the actions that would be required to move GMI from its current malaise to the new state of industry leadership. Linker at this point brought forward the straw man strategies created by the task force for consideration and adaptation. Much discussion and debate led finally to the identification of specific actions and investments that would be required. These were grouped according to basic operating objectives and evolved into six change programs to be further defined during Phase 2 of the journey:

GMI Mission Statement

To be the preferred global supplier of high-value-added product components and services in our chosen market segments

Demand Generation

- Customer accounts managed globally
- Value-based product pricing
- Cost-effective information sharing
- Demand management and scheduling
- Lowest total delivered cost
- Business cost model drives customer value proposition

Demand Fulfillment

- Flexible factory capacity
- Cross-qualified plants and workers
- One-piece flow, cell manufacturing
- Optimized, low-cost production
- JIT inventory management
- Global supply partnerships
- Capable and motivated employees

Product and Process Innovation

- Fastest in new product development
- World leader in advanced materials
- Reuse of standard components in design
- Redesign driven by performance data
- Standardized CAD software
- Collaborative design with customers and suppliers

Figure 3.5. The Future Vision for GMI.

- Speed product development.
- Enhance business infrastructure.
- Achieve manufacturing excellence.
- Delight the customer.
- Build best people.
- Assure supply quality.

The executive team agreed on relative priorities among the goals as well as on the more specific projects shown in Figure 3.6. A preliminary draft of priorities and timing for these program projects was further documented, as shown in Figure 3.7.

From this plan of action, the sequence, timing, and magnitude of required investments were established, and program benefits were forecast. Although these figures were approximations, they were considered sufficiently accurate to estimate the cash flows that could be expected. A preliminary business case was thus formulated and a projected net present value for the entire journey was calculated—in excess of $2 billion. Although this figure was only an estimate, it created substantial enthusiasm among executive management. And although the rough numbers used to calculate the estimate would need to be refined during detailed design stage in the next phase of the journey, it was now clear to everyone that there would indeed be a next phase.

At the end of the third day, the change team presented a strategic architecture document that summarized the current situation, strategic direction, and ultimate business vision. Figure 3.8 reproduces that document in skeletal form. (The actual document included the details shown in Figures 3.2 through 3.6, as well as the quantitative measure of expected performance improvement and the business case that forecast the costs and benefits.) The strategic architecture confirmed for all present that the pieces of planning fit together. Berger at this point extracted a public commitment from his management team to return to their organizations and share the new vision with their direct reports.

Speed Product Development
- Establish advanced materials group.
- Reengineer product development process for flexibility.
- Focus redesign on speed and responsiveness.
- Involve customers and suppliers in new product design.
- Enhance project management skills for new products.

Enhance Business Infrastructure
- Improve our ability to monitor and control operations.
- Redesign business interfaces to lower overhead costs.
- Standardize data definition and financial reporting.
- Install common ERP platform worldwide.
- Reestablish I/T competency base.
- Standardize computing platform.

Achieve Manufacturing Excellence
- Identify and share global best practices.
- Apply one-piece flow and cellular manufacturing.
- Drive continuous improvement through total quality.
- Establish performance management system.
- Create rapid-response build-to-order capability.
- Deploy methodology for project management.

Delight the Customer
- Create customer relationship management function.
- Establish customer council.
- Develop effective customer call center support.
- Implement customer data warehouse and mining ability.
- Improve salesforce recruitment, development, and retention.

Build Best People
- Establish a comprehensive management education program.
- Design an effective rewards and recognition program.
- Use performance system to change behavior.
- Implement team leader development model.
- Develop processes to improve employee selection.

Assure Supply Quality
- Source materials based upon strategic partnerships.
- Implement real-time operational linkages to partners.
- Ensure supplier involvement in reengineering.
- Establish technology council.
- Support key suppliers in process improvement.
- Conduct annual supplier review to track and measure value.

Figure 3.6. GMI-2004 Development Plan.

	1997				1998				1999				2000				2001				2002				2003				2004			
	1st	2nd	3rd	4th	1st	2nd	3rd	4th	1st	2nd	3rd	4th	1st	2nd	3rd	4th	1st	2nd	3rd	4th	1st	2nd	3rd	4th	1st	2nd	3rd	4th	1st	2nd	3rd	4th

Delight the Customer
- Create customer relationship management function.
- Establish customer council.
- Improve salesforce recruitment, development, and retention.
- Develop effective customer call center support.
- Develop customer data warehouse and mining capability.
- Establish single common GMI-customer interface.

Speed Product Development
- Reengineer product development process for flexibility.
- Focus product redesign process on speed and responsiveness.
- Establish advanced materials group.
- Enhance project management skills for new product development.
- Involve customers and suppliers in new product design.

Enhance Business Infrastructure
- Develop a plan to reestablish I/T competency base.
- Partner with strategic I/T service providers.
- Standardize data definitions and financial reporting system.
- Improve ability to monitor and control local operations.
- Redesign business interfaces to reduce transaction costs.
- Install a common ERP platform worldwide.

Figure 3.7. GMI-2004 Implementation Plan.

	1997				1998				1999				2000				2001				2002				2003				2004			
	1st	2nd	3rd	4th	1st	2nd	3rd	4th	1st	2nd	3rd	4th	1st	2nd	3rd	4th	1st	2nd	3rd	4th	1st	2nd	3rd	4th	1st	2nd	3rd	4th	1st	2nd	3rd	4th

Achieve Manufacturing Excellence
- Establish GMI manufacturing council.
- Identify and share global best practices.
- Drive continuous improvement through total quality.
- Establish performance measurement system.
- Deploy methodology for project management.
- Apply one-piece flow and cellular manufacturing.

Build Best People
- Develop GMI management education program.
- Develop process to improve employee selection, development, and retention.
- Develop a reward and recognition system aligned with strategy.
- Improve team leader development program.
- Use performance system to change behavior.

Assure Quality Supply
- Establish a supply-chain council.
- Ensure supplier participation in GMI reengineering.
- Support key suppliers in process improvement.
- Source materials based on strategic partnerships.
- Implement real-time operational linkages to partners.

Figure 3.7. GMI-2004 Implementation Plan, Cont'd.

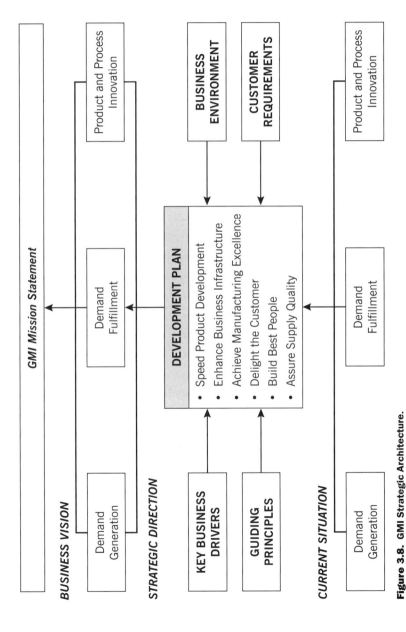

BUSINESS VISION

GMI Mission Statement

Product and Process Innovation

Demand Fulfillment

Demand Generation

STRATEGIC DIRECTION

BUSINESS ENVIRONMENT

CUSTOMER REQUIREMENTS

DEVELOPMENT PLAN

- Speed Product Development
- Enhance Business Infrastructure
- Achieve Manufacturing Excellence
- Delight the Customer
- Build Best People
- Assure Supply Quality

KEY BUSINESS DRIVERS

GUIDING PRINCIPLES

CURRENT SITUATION

Product and Process Innovation

Demand Fulfillment

Demand Generation

Figure 3.8. GMI Strategic Architecture.

Having participated in this three-day process of defining a vision supported by planning, the executive team was now on board, both openly embracing and publicly supporting the new business vision for GMI.

Your Analysis

1. By the end of the retreat, had the leaders created the four basic elements of a business vision?
2. What further progress has Linker achieved regarding executive consensus, support, and commitment? How has he done it? What more is needed?
3. To what extent is information technology now an issue in this phase of the journey? If it is not the central issue, what importance does it bear?
4. Where do information technology concerns show up in the Development Plan of Figure 3.6?
5. How well is GMI doing thus far along the journey? What needs to be done next?

Assessment of the Strategy Definition

To this point, Linker's process for developing GMI's new business strategy has been textbook perfect. He has created readiness within the organization by documenting clear examples of unacceptable performance. He has dampened resistance to new proposals and future changes by involving credible members of the organization in the data collection process. Further, he has enabled and encouraged these team members to present the task force finding to their colleagues in nonthreatening forums, and he has solicited feedback from the organization with which he has tested the task force findings and conclusions.

Does GMI Have a Vision?
Clearly at this point Linker has established the motivation for
and objectives of the GMI-2004 journey. He has taken steps to develop a preliminary business case with an expected payoff in excess of $2 billion. He has documented a strategic architecture for
GMI (Figure 3.8) to summarize the current situation, the development plan, and the vision of future operations. This document
provides a high-level description not only of GMI's business architecture as the journey begins in 1997, but also of business
processes planned to evolve by 2004. Obviously this architecture
must remain a living document, since unanticipated events will
surely arise in the months and years ahead. This guide must
adapt and adjust as the journey progresses, assumptions evolve,
and new facts emerge.

Continuing Work on Support and Commitment
Linker's involvement of executive management in the design
and refinement of the strategy has gone a long way toward building the commitment of top managers to the plan that has been
developed. But the energy and enthusiasm of a three-day planning retreat can quickly dissipate as it meets the immediate demands of day-to-day operations. Executive understanding and
commitment to the actions implied by the plan face a serious test
as these managers take the results of the retreat and present them
to subordinates in the following weeks. Not everyone who needs
to be is yet on board with GMI-2004. The explanation and selling
of the vision to the rest of GMI's management team and employees will be a critical element for the success of the journey.

Is This About I/T Infrastructure?
The formulation phase of the GMI-2004 journey continues to
transcend the issue of I/T infrastructure. While I/T is the essential focus of the "Enhance Business Infrastructure," part of

the program, it appears only indirectly as an enabling element in the other programs outlined in Figure 3.6. "Delight the Customer," for example, will require GMI to investigate I/T investments in an "available-to-promise" capability for order entry, a call center support system for customer service, and new data warehousing and mining competencies for market analysis.

Progress to Date

By June 1997, Harry Linker had successfully guided the GMI management team through a comprehensive planning process and had begun to create within the firm a readiness for change. Together he and the management team had defined a new strategic vision and performance goals for GMI, and they had identified the business capabilities that would be needed to achieve them. The work of creating these new business capabilities had been divided into manageable projects and the infrastructure investments needed to support them had been identified. Finally, the newly proposed business strategy and its financial implications had been documented in the form of a business case. The journey was off to an excellent start.

SUMMARY

In this chapter we began to present the case of GMI through the lens of the Journey Management and Business Architecture models. GMI had previously responded to falling revenues with reengineering strategies based on no real diagnosis of the problem or the company's competitive position and current operations.

Brett Berger, the new CEO, launched a process akin to the formulation phase of journey management by placing a man experienced with successful change at the head of GMI's new effort to change. As the new CFO, Harry Linker not only recruited an effective task force but also worked hard from the start to ensure that Berger and his executive team would learn about the basic problems, buy in to the need to solve them, and provide open support and commitment.

Linker's team spent three months on Business Diagnosis, touring every part of the company to answer key factual questions about the current state of GMI: current strategies, external environment, performance compared with the competition, pressures for change, benefits of change, and managerial recognition of the need for change. Linker paid special attention to achieving executive management consensus, developing the support of sponsors, and gathering a capable, cross-functional team for change.

Linker's team analyzed GMI's current weaknesses in its three core business processes. It also began to consider solutions. Moving to the Strategy Definition step of Phase 1, the team carried its ideas out to individual company executives. Next the task force brought its analysis and recommendations to an intensive, three-day retreat for Berger and his management team. Through a careful, step-by-step process, Linker guided the retreat in converting his straw man solutions into an authentic, fact-based vision: business strategy, performance targets, operating plan, and business case. Having reshaped and refined the ideas brought by the task force, the executive team now gave strong support to a six-part development plan, much of which would depend on new information technologies and skills.

Questions for Consideration

1. Have you had experiences analogous to those described in this chapter for Brett Berger or Harry Linker? What similarities do you see between your experience and theirs? What differences?
2. How have management retreats that you've attended resembled or differed from the retreat that Linker organized?
3. To what extent has this chapter been about information technology? Where has it shown up in the work of Linker and his task force?
4. So far, how successful do you expect the company to be at achieving its goals for GMI-2004?
5. Suppose you were part of a similar task force for your own company? What ideas does this chapter suggest about how you might want to handle Phase 1 of the Journey Management Model?

Preparing and Implementing Projects

H arry Linker, GMI's CFO, got the GMI executive management team off to a good start in developing a strategy for organizational change—essentially following
Phase 1 of the Journey Management Model, the phase of strategy formulation. Using a comprehensive planning process he
gathered facts that documented GMI's precarious competitive
position and created a readiness for change within the team.
Together he and the GMI executive team defined a new strategic vision and performance goals for the company, and identified the business capabilities that would be needed to achieve
them. The work of building the new business capabilities was
divided into programs, and the proposed business strategy and

its financial implications were organized in the form of a business case for the journey, which they named GMI-2004.

In this chapter, we pick up the GMI case in the preparation phase of GMI-2004, focusing on a few pivotal events and interactions among activities that enable, create, or depend on a new I/T infrastructure. Although the implementation of GMI's ERP system, for example, might be viewed in isolation as a technical program to install new computer software, it must be linked to the goals of the strategic journey if senior management is to view the investment as a success.

■ Phases 2 and 3 for Projects to Build Infrastructure

The Journey Management Model calls for programs to be specified in Phase 2, then implemented by the execution of *projects* during Phase 3. Projects are coordinated at a program level to manage the contention for resources that will occur among implementation activities that affect common business functions, facilities, equipment, schedules, or people. Because of constraints on such resources, it's usually impossible to launch all programs simultaneously. Instead, some programs will start and even complete implementation before others begin preparation.

A Second Transitional Assessment

The transition between the Journey Management Phase 1 (Formulation) and Phase 2 (Preparation) offers a second natural opportunity to assess the organization's readiness to move forward. Nine management questions are key to continued success. At the Journey Management level one asks:

- Do the journey sponsors remain committed to the strategic vision and business case?

- Do the facts and assumptions that drive the strategy and its business case remain valid?
- Are the business capabilities needed to achieve the strategic vision and business case adequately defined?
- Will the planned infrastructure and process changes deliver these business capabilities?
- Is the journey subdivided into manageable programs that deliver these infrastructure and process changes?

In addition, at the Program Management level one asks:

- Does line management understand and support the strategic vision and program goals?
- Is there a common understanding of the new operating plan and its business process implications?
- Does the business case identify the size and timing of program costs and benefits and create sufficient value to constitute an obvious imperative for the proposed changes?
- Has a performance plan to measure program achievement against the business case been shared, understood, and accepted, and has it been linked to the compensation and reward system?

Even though they're not formally using the model, Linker and his task force have successfully addressed each of these questions. Note that if any question could not be answered affirmatively, then it would be advisable to revisit the formulation steps of Phase 1 to resolve the problem. Otherwise, moving forward would carry a significant likelihood of failure. For GMI in June 1997, however, all these pieces appear to be in place.

Determining Program and Project Precedence

What programs and projects should be done first? Figure 3.7 showed the initial schedule that was laid out for GMI-2004. It's useful to take a moment now to consider the thinking behind that order.

The sequencing of implementation work must strike a balance in the competing dimensions of project urgency, visibility, speed, cost, payback, leverage, natural prerequisites, and required resources. The allocation of resources here is often less about acquiring additional resources to support the planned work than it is about freeing up resources that already exist—in other words, deciding what ongoing work will be discontinued and therefore what resources are no longer needed to support it. Likewise, the setting of the pace of program execution is governed less by the amount of money that might be made available than by the rate at which the journey can effectively use that money. Suppose for the moment that all funds and resources needed by GMI-2004 were available immediately: the company still couldn't take on all the process development at once. The amount of change involved in moving GMI from where it was in 1997 to where it needed to go is so large that the organization could not survive the shock of so massive a change in such a short period of time.

Because the business strategy and performance improvement goals established by the GMI management team are ambitious, no quick fixes to GMI's marketing, logistics, or manufacturing systems can achieve them. New infrastructure will have to be built before the reengineering of GMI's core processes can be reasonably attempted. Linker understands that substantial investments in organization and process infrastructure will be needed in advance of the planned business process changes. However, he knows that the payback on much of this needed investment will require a longer period than the three-year limit to which the company has been accustomed. The projects that would actually change the core business processes are not scheduled to begin for two years or more.

Thus one might reasonably be concerned that real organizational resistance to GMI-2004 will not surface until changes to core business processes are actually required and that in the intervening period the consensus reached recently by senior management will dissipate. In addition, Berger may not have three or four years to deliver improvement in his operating performance. At minimum, therefore, Linker will have to be clear with Berger regarding the nature and timing of journey "deliverables" and then actively manage both the CEO's expectations and those of the board of directors.

Given the operating plan that was developed in 1997 during Phase 1—Formulation of the GMI-2004 journey, four key questions need to be answered now by Linker and his team during the capability analysis stage of Phase 2—Preparation:

- What specific business process changes will be required to achieve the new operating plan?
- What process infrastructure changes (information and production) will therefore be required?
- What organization infrastructure changes (structure, governance, and competence) will be needed?
- How will the visible measures of performance encourage management and workforce support?

In answering these questions Linker's team would soon identify competency and governance deficiencies in GMI's organization infrastructure, as well as severe I/T deficiencies in its process infrastructure. As a result, infrastructure projects to address these deficiencies would be launched first on the GMI-2004 journey.

On the Move (June 1997–August 1998)

As Linker considered the sequence in which the six programs of GMI-2004 and their component projects should be started, he recognized that GMI's current infrastructures for management accounting, information technology, and human resources were woefully inadequate to support the proposed operating plan of GMI-2004. These problems would have to be corrected before the planned changes to business processes could begin. So with executive support for the new business strategy firmly in place, Linker focused first on GMI's organization infrastructure, where competency and governance deficiencies needed to be addressed. As a result GMI-2004 led off with programs to "Build Best People" and "Enhance Business Infrastructure" noted in the schedule shown in Figure 3.7.

Educating GMI's Managers

For the lead project in the "Build Best People" program, Linker partnered with Human Resources to educate management about ways to improve employee attitudes and to develop needed process skills within the company. Both preparation and implementation were straightforward for this project. Gaps were identified in GMI's managerial competencies, and nine education courses were designed to fill those gaps and delivered with the help of a local university: Information Systems, Management Accounting, Process Reengineering, Team Building, Total Quality Management, Operational Excellence, Strategic Planning, Industrial Marketing, and Increased Human Effectiveness. Courses were hosted in-house and made available to GMI's top three hundred managers as needed. The courses provided not only an opportunity to establish concepts and build vocabulary among GMI's top management but also a forum to debate proposed actions and to discuss the ramifications of these actions. Berger's well-publicized intention to attend each of these classes assured full participation by the rest of the GMI management team. This in turn assured that the new ideas and vocabulary spread quickly throughout the company. Out of a nine-month education process emerged a new spirit of teamwork and optimism as personal and professional relationships were formed and common problems and concerns were identified.

Preparing New Organizational Infrastructure

A second infrastructure project took more time. Linker needed help from outside GMI to install a new standardized financial reporting system. And prior to that he needed to rebuild the company's I/T infrastructure. His objective was to revamp GMI management processes by increasing management's ability to see into and control business unit operations.

During his three-month review of business unit operations, Linker had uncovered a potpourri of financial systems that lacked integration and suffered from decades of uncoordinated enhancement efforts. The general ledger system, for example, was the one application that everyone could count on to run reliably every week. Therefore, whenever a new report was required to address a current management concern, a new sub-account in the ledger was created to capture the needed data. The resulting chart-of-accounts was too complex for anyone to understand. Moreover, dozens of cost accountants using hundreds of spreadsheets were needed each month to reconcile accounts and close the books. For Linker's plans for streamlined operations and cross-functional cooperation to succeed, all accounting transactions would have to be transparent. All managers would have to understand how operations worked within the company and trust that the accounting systems were fairly reflecting the consequences of their actions and decisions.

Before a new financial reporting system could be created, however, GMI's I/T capabilities would need to be strengthened. Linker could see that GMI's current information systems could not support the organization infrastructure improvements that were needed. He recognized also that the current Data Processing staff, as the group was known internally, was not up to carrying out the large-scale system development that was going to be needed. To document the nature and extent of GMI's I/T problems, he commissioned the firm of ABC-Consulting to perform an I/T assessment. ABC was a highly regarded international consulting company known for its abilities in the design and implementation of computer-based business systems.

Keith Cunningham, an experienced Information Systems Strategy partner, led the ABC-Consulting team that arrived at GMI in the summer of 1997. As he and his team performed their review, they discovered a corporate I/T organization in disarray, suffering from years of neglect. The corporation had no common I/T systems architecture (that is, no standards for hardware, software, data, and communication systems), no formal system development methodology, and no procedures to link the I/T budget and development priorities to the business strategy and its implied operating plans. There was a documented four-year backlog of I/T project requests to modify or replace a portfolio of nearly nine hundred COBOL applications, and there was insufficient talent and personnel to address this need. To make matters worse, the I/T staff was pigeonholed into dozens of old, overcrowded cubicles spread out on multiple floors in four separate buildings. There was a total of seventy-three full-time professional positions at corporate headquarters with no personnel management to speak of. There was no performance appraisal system, no way to measure individual development, and no formal training program. Salaries and benefits were 18 percent below the regional average. The median age of an I/T professional was forty-nine and the annual turnover of new hires was a staggering 40 percent. All important system development projects for the past ten years had been contracted out to one of several consulting companies that regularly did work for GMI. In short, the I/T organization was in a shambles.

As Cunningham developed his report and recommendations, he worked closely with Harry Linker. Cunningham was intimately familiar with Linker's GMI-2004 change agenda and clearly understood its need for a modern I/T infrastructure. He therefore presented his recommendations to GMI in the form of a long-term I/T strategy called *Global Systems 2004*, which both paralleled and supported Linker's business strategy. His report detailed the dismal state of data processing at GMI and warned that the company had fallen dangerously behind the industry in its ability to support the business capabilities required to remain competitive in the emerging world of e-business. Both Harry Linker and the CEO, Brett Berger, were impressed by the detail and logic of the report and by the strength and passion of Cunningham's presentation to GMI's management team. They quickly concluded that Keith Cunningham was exactly the right man to lead the I/T function at GMI, and within three weeks he was presented with a very attractive financial package. After some reflection, Cunningham accepted the offer and assumed the new corporate role of Chief Information Officer (CIO), reporting to Harry Linker.

Preparing a New I/T Infrastructure
How and how fast should these I/T deficiencies be corrected? Issues of task priority, project pace, and resource commitment needed to be considered as part of scheduling the I/T program. (This is a component of what we would call the *detailed design* stage of Phase 2, Preparation.) Seven questions are relevant for all programs at this point:

- Has the program been broken into manageable projects, with appropriate precedence, that achieve measurable goals in a reasonable period?
- How do program projects combine to deliver the planned infrastructure or business capabilities?
- Is there an integrated plan to build, test, and deploy each planned capability?
- Are the roles and responsibilities needed to achieve the capabilities established?
- Have the key employees and other resources required by the project been identified?
- Are there project milestones at which to assess progress and the need for adjustments?
- Do performance metrics motivate desired individual and team-level behavior?

In his new role of CIO, Keith Cunningham began the implementation of Global Systems 2004 in January 1998 and established the schedule of project activities laid out in Figure 4.1. The

	1998				1999				2000				2001				2002				2003				2004			
	1st	2nd	3rd	4th	1st	2nd	3rd	4th	1st	2nd	3rd	4th	1st	2nd	3rd	4th	1st	2nd	3rd	4th	1st	2nd	3rd	4th	1st	2nd	3rd	4th

Platform
- Establish hardware architecture.
- Confirm Year 2000 (Y2K) software readiness.
- Select an ERP software standard.
- Design network architecture.
- Establish hardware and software standards for desktop computing.

Processes
- Design I/T staff training and continue education programs.
- Cultivate and develop university relationships.
- Select project management methodology.
- Launch three-day executive I/T seminar for top three hundred.
- Establish I/T steering committee.
- Link I/T budget and priorities to business sponsors and strategy.

Resources
- Inventory hardware, software, data, and skills.
- Rationalize and consolidate facilities.
- Launch university recruiting initiative.
- Partner with a prime systems consulting firm.
- Establish adequate I/T budget and staffing authorization.
- Build internal ERP capabilities.

	1998				1999				2000				2001				2002				2003				2004			
	1st	2nd	3rd	4th	1st	2nd	3rd	4th	1st	2nd	3rd	4th	1st	2nd	3rd	4th	1st	2nd	3rd	4th	1st	2nd	3rd	4th	1st	2nd	3rd	4th

ERP Conversion

- Standardize general ledger worldwide.
- Launch basic HR application portfolio.
- Install production maintance application upon request.
- Establish shared global designs (SGD) for operations.
- Launch logistics and manufacturing in United States.
- Sales and Marketing United States
- Logistics and manufacturing Europe
- Sales and Marketing Europe
- Rest of world
- Rest of world

Figure 4.1. Global Systems 2004 Implementation Schedule.

start dates of these activities were set to mirror the GMI-2004 implementation plan. Some elements of the schedule would likely be adjusted in the months ahead to reflect the actual progress of the GMI-2004 programs that were being supported.

With clear sponsorship from Brett Berger and Harry Linker, these projects moved forward in rapid succession, and the company and its management digested these changes faster than Cunningham originally believed possible. He established a corporate standard for desktop computing, redesigned and outsourced the corporate communications network, and began the transition to a new client-server computing platform. He also orchestrated a thorough study of ERP packages (Oracle, SAP, Baan, J D Edwards, and PeopleSoft) from which SAP's product R/3 emerged as having the best match of software capabilities to the business process needs envisioned by GMI-2004.

With the tacit concurrence of the business unit heads, a corporate edict was issued: "If an operating unit decides to buy any new business software application, then it will be selected from the SAP R/3 family of solutions." In addition, it was agreed that operating procedures implemented via the new software would "comply with corporate standards for core business processes except when precluded by local regulations or strategic necessity." Cunningham believed that this agreement would have the Darwinian effect of evolving business processes over time to a common platform of system software and operating procedures. And this would pay dividends in the form of dramatically lower software maintenance costs, stronger financial controls, improved process reliability, reduced operating expenses, shared best practices, interchangeability of personnel (across facilities and business units), and a common unified interface to customers and suppliers.

Major changes eventually implemented through August 1999 included the following:

- Doubling the I/T operating budget from 1.5 percent to 3.1 percent of revenues.
- Selecting SAP as the sole ERP software vendor for all new business system implementations.
- Implementing SAP R/3 modules for financial accounting, human resource management, and production maintenance, as the first step in replacing the existing tangle of largely un-documented COBOL applications.
- Designing and constructing a corporate intranet built on a new LAN and WAN communications environment, whose operation had been outsourced to ATT.
- Replacing a mainframe-centric IBM computing platform with client-server architecture based on HP, Dell, and Toshiba hardware.
- Establishing a company-wide standard for desktop computing (Intel processors, Windows NT operating system, Microsoft Office 97, Internet Explorer, Lotus Notes, and TCP/IP communications).
- Completing Year-2000 software remediation and successfully testing the results.
- Rolling out a formal college-recruiting program to attract qualified I/T analysts, designers, and programmers.
- Increasing the corporate I/T professional staff from 73 to 97 with an authorization to grow to 121.
- Launching construction of a $7 million office facility within the GMI headquarters complex to bring the I/T staff to-gether in one location.
- Creating a continuing education and tuition reimbursement program for current I/T staff.
- Working with a nationally recognized university to develop a three-day management education seminar, Strategic Uses of Information Technology, aimed at GMI's senior executives and business unit managers.

- Establishing a corporate I/T steering committee to review I/T budget requests and to establish priorities for I/T investments.
- Developing a working document that spelled out roles and responsibilities during design and implementation of new information systems for both functional managers and I/T staff.

For more than a year Cunningham and his staff worked to prepare the technical foundation required for a corporate-wide ERP system. When fully implemented the operating logic of the ERP system would embody the strategic changes planned for GMI's business processes. This ERP system conversion would be the largest, most expensive, and potentially most dangerous resource investment in the history of the company. It had to be prepared for and executed with care.

Your Analysis

1. What was the role that management education project played in the GMI-2004 journey?
2. Why did a major investment in I/T infrastructure take center stage during the journey?
3. How was the I/T investment plan developed and then implemented?

Assessment of Basic Infrastructure Requirements

Linker's team quickly identified competence and governance deficiencies within GMI's organization infrastructure, as well as I/T deficiencies within its process infrastructure. Both infrastructures would have to be strengthened before serious work on business process changes could commence.

The Role of Management Education in the Journey
Linker's decision to partner early and at length with Human Resources and a local university on a major management education project tells us how important he considered the problem

of *management competence* to be. We concur. From his organizational interviews, Linker could see that GMI's top three hundred managers had been focusing so much and so long on marginal improvements to existing processes that they had lost both their skill and appetite for large-scale change. He needed to reenergize this group since these were the people who would actually drive the new strategy throughout the company, and they would have to feel comfortable with the business concepts implicit in the new strategy before they could champion it. Successful execution of the management education project was an important first step in strengthening organization infrastructure by rebuilding management competence and bolstering management support for the coming business transformation.

Rationale for I/T Infrastructure Investment
The need for a major investment in I/T infrastructure arose from a void in organization governance. For the new operating plan of streamlined operations and cross-functional cooperation to succeed, all accounting transactions would have to be transparent. Every manager would have to understand how financial operations worked within the company and trust that the accounting systems were fairly reflecting the consequences of every action and decision. But GMI had a chart-of-accounts that no one could understand. Moreover, to track the progress of GMI-2004, management would need an improved ability to monitor business unit operating performance. Linker clearly had to do something about both problems.

A standardized set of financial applications established across all business units worldwide would address both needs. But GMI's I/T competency and process infrastructure would have to be rebuilt in advance of this deployment. GMI's I/T function was inadequately staffed in June 1997 to support the development of Linker's financial applications and the other business process software needed for the new operating plan.

I/T competence would have to be reestablished and organization structure choices, such as insourcing or outsourcing of specific I/T capabilities, would have to be made. Thus to support business process changes within GMI, a major I/T investment took center stage in the GMI-2004 journey.

Developing and Implementing the Plan for I/T Investment
Because Linker knew that his team lacked the technical expertise to make informed decisions in the I/T arena, he sensibly reached outside the company for help in developing an I/T investment plan. A thorough process of capability analysis, conducted by a well-known and highly regarded consulting firm, documented an I/T organization in disarray: overcommitted, understaffed, and poorly managed, with low morale and high turnover. Much work needed to be done to acquire needed human resources, to rebuild an inadequate computing platform, and to establish sound I/T management processes. The analysis provided the evidence required by the board to fund the necessary investment. In turn, this led to the hiring of Keith Cunningham as CIO.

We believe that Cunningham's plan to reestablish I/T competencies and infrastructure in support of GMI-2004 was aggressive but achievable. Undoubtedly, factors that affected the design of the schedule included the natural prerequisites among tasks, the pending disasters that demanded attention, and the need for early visible successes that could build momentum for the program. Since speed was of the essence, Cunningham reasonably decided to purchase a standard suite of ERP modules that could be installed relatively quickly, rather than build the application software needed to support the new business processes from scratch. And to assure management's comprehension of what his plan entailed, he complemented the program schedule (which established project sequence and timing) with supporting documentation that detailed program scope and required resources, as well as responsibilities for achieving intermediate milestones and delivering final business results.

Cunningham correctly focused initially on defining an I/T architecture. The common hardware, network, and system software standards that this established would greatly simplify the later work of business systems software implementation. By late 1998, he had established a corporate standard for desktop computing, redesigned and outsourced the corporate communications network, and begun the transition to a new client-server computing platform. He rebuilt the I/T physical plant and developed roles, responsibilities, and management controls over I/T budgets and investments. Finally, he established SAP R/3 as the global standard for all application development. The sum of these projects positioned GMI to implement business process changes that would enhance revenues, reduce expenses, and thus recoup the I/T investment.

In summary, GMI got off to an excellent start in 1998. Working from the business strategy and operating plan developed during formulation, Linker's team performed a comprehensive capability analysis. By focusing on business process changes that would be required to achieve the GMI-2004 operating plan, the team quickly identified gaps in organization and process infrastructure. Linker judiciously leveraged key resources from outside his team to address these deficiencies. First, he partnered with Human Resources and a local university to educate management about ways to improve employee attitudes and to develop needed process skills within the company. A new management education program was thus implemented. Additionally, Linker sought help from outside the company to build an I/T platform that would support the new business processes of GMI-2004. He engaged ABC-Consulting to devise a plan to rebuild GMI's I/T infrastructure and subsequently hired Keith Cunningham to execute that plan. With this foundation in place, Linker's team made steady progress on their plan during the months that followed.

■ Phase 3—Implementation of Business Process Changes

By September 1998, with the construction of supporting I/T infrastructure far enough along, it was time for GMI's management to begin implementing the new business processes implied by the GMI-2004 operating plan. SAP R/3 would be used as the vehicle for installing the planned changes. The entire effort worldwide was scheduled to take five years. It would begin in the United States and extend through Europe and Asia, first for administrative and support processes and later for marketing, logistics, and manufacturing.

A Third Transitional Assessment

At the beginning of every significant program project, sixteen questions are key to determining the continued success of the journey, all of which add up to asking, "Is this project as planned still aligned with the current business strategy, and is the organization ready to move forward?" At the Journey Management level one again asks,

- Do the journey sponsors remain committed to the strategic vision and business case?
- Do the facts and assumptions that drive the strategy and its business case remain valid?
- Are the business capabilities needed to achieve the strategic vision and business case adequately defined?
- Will the planned infrastructure and process changes deliver planned business capabilities?
- Is the journey broken into manageable programs that deliver these infrastructure and process changes?

At the level of Program Management, though, one is concerned with these questions:

- Does management continue to demonstrate active support for the program?
- Have "quick win" project opportunities been identified and implemented?
- Have changes in facts and assumptions been reviewed for impact on program plans?
- Have the strategy, operating plan, and business case been revalidated against changes?
- Have changes in program scope been documented and appropriately rebudgeted?
- Have feedback processes been used to manage program budgets and sponsor expectations?

At the level of Project Management, finally, one now asks,

- Do clear project specifications define project scope and the time and resources required?
- Have key employees and needed resources been committed to the project on a sustained basis?
- Can the project team members articulate the business value that the project will achieve?
- Is there a specific plan to assess line management against the project objectives and do they understand and accept those objectives?
- Will the workforce understand and accept the resulting infrastructure and process changes?

A failure to achieve satisfactory answers to these questions should return the project team to the appropriate stage in Phase 1 or Phase 2 to resolve the problem identified. But for the GMI-2004 journey in September 1998, everything was in order. Linker and Cunningham had covered all the bases, even though they were working without a formal framework.

Getting Down to Cases (September 1998–November 1999)

With sufficient I/T infrastructure in place by September 1998, the work of rolling out SAP R/3 modules into the business units began. It started slowly as the Global Systems 2004 team gathered its initial implementation experience. To ensure a success, the opening projects had to be selected with care.

Carefully Selecting the Lead Projects

Cunningham knew that there are basically three ways in which ERP technology can be moved into an established corporation such as GMI:

Complete customization is an every-business-for-itself approach where independent ERP modules based on separate software and databases are installed in each operating unit on an as-needed basis. Only modest linkages across the enterprise are established via a few non-core processes such as financial reporting or employee benefits. This approach suits an organization with either a decentralized management philosophy or a collection of business units that share few common products, processes, or customers. It entails both larger initial development costs and much higher residual maintenance expense than other approaches, as new versions of the various underlying ERP software packages are released over time and the customization process must be repeated.

Forced march is a process in which a corporate edict directs an immediate standardization and linkage of all legacy systems across the entire enterprise. Only modest deviations from the corporate standards are permitted and only when a clear business case can be presented to justify the variance. Development and maintenance costs here are substantially lower, but this draconian procedure works well for only the smallest of companies or those facing an obviously compelling business necessity such as the pending collapse of current operations.

Targets of opportunity is a process by which a set of standard software modules from a single ERP vendor is installed quickly into an organization that is highly motivated to accept it. Typically, this situation arises when either the standard software closely matches existing business processes and therefore meets little organizational resistance, or the existing processes are so obviously inadequate for some immediate business requirement that the new software is embraced as providing a tested and desired best practice that solves the current problem. Development and maintenance costs here are minimized.

Of these three paths, the least desirable from Cunningham's perspective was complete customization. This approach would yield few synergies across the company and create a complex and expensive maintenance legacy as the customization would have to be repeated with each new release of the underlying ERP software. The company could wind up with an enormous program cost while gaining little of its potential benefits. Cunningham's preference was to begin the conversion process by focusing on targets of opportunity, in which a business unit would be willing to adapt its operating processes to match the natural capabilities of the SAP software. Not only would this reduce later maintenance costs, but by working with organizations that were motivated to see him succeed, he could reduce implementation risk. It would also afford him the luxury of moving the implementation forward at a controlled pace as he cultivated a base of experience and skill in the I/T function. A forced march, on the other hand, would overwhelm the existing capacity of his I/T staff and would force heavy reliance on external consultants. It would also create organizational resistance on so many fronts that it would be difficult to manage the entire effort.

Even though Cunningham felt he had picked the best software for the job when he selected SAP R/3, he did not expect that it would be easy to implement the new ERP system. Many of the benefits associated with the ERP conversion would accrue outside the individual businesses. And getting those business unit managers to give up their current operating procedures and install what they considered to be "new computer software" was bound to be a hard sell. The SAP conversion costs would have to be capitalized or expensed, as appropriate, in the financial statements of the business units. And this would have the effect of lowering the units' RONA performance and therefore lowering salary bonuses. Thus—despite a multiyear backlog of maintenance requests for their current software—business unit managers were bound to be reluctant to commit themselves to the financial cost and organizational trauma of a full-blown ERP conversion.

Cunningham understood that a corporate mandate might eventually be required to encourage movement by pockets of resistance who refused to embrace the new technology, but this was not that moment. He chose instead to begin the SAP transition with a selection of targets of opportunity.

First Target of Opportunity: Financial Reporting

The first opportunity to install a planned set of SAP modules arrived in September 1998. For nearly six months, CFO Harry Linker had been impressing upon all who would listen the critical role that a standardized chart-of-accounts would play in supporting the strategic goals of GMI-2004. Through a series of spirited meetings with his international controllers, punctuated intermittently with arm-twisting and martinis, he was able to hammer out an agreement in principle on a draft system of data definitions and coding and a chart-of-accounts that appeared workable. It was time to try it out.

Organizational learning about the SAP R/3 technology thus began in September 1998 with R/3's accounting modules as part of Linker's financial reporting project, called *Financials 2000*. Linker wanted to roll out the suite of standardized SAP financial applications across all business units worldwide to enhance management's ability to monitor business unit operating performance. The goals of this project were

- To establish standard data definitions and financial reporting across all regions and operating locations
- To improve the ability of local managers to monitor and control their operations
- To enable rapid and accurate financial consolidations for the corporation
- To achieve a badly needed corporate-level view into local operations

Building an SAP Skill Base Within GMI

Cunningham viewed the Financials 2000 project not as an end in itself but rather as the beginning both of an SAP implementation process that would last for the next five years and of a software maintenance commitment that would persist for long after that. A fundamental I/T strategy issue therefore needed to be addressed: Where should the expertise to design, install, and maintain these new ERP systems reside? Should the skill set be developed and maintained within GMI or should these capabilities be outsourced to a third party? Cunningham believed strongly that the ability to customize business systems quickly would be key to achieving the operational objectives of adaptability and agility set forth in the GMI-2004 strategy. He further believed that it was critical to maintain the SAP skill base within the company, and he therefore laid plans to develop one.

With approval from Berger and assistance from Linker, Cunningham assembled a group of fourteen bright, energetic high-performance employees (six from I/T and eight from the business units). They were to form the nucleus of an implementation team that, beginning with Financials 2000, would lead the deployment of all SAP R/3 modules throughout the company over the next five years. To begin the team's training and skill development process, Cunningham contracted with his old firm, ABC-Consulting. He negotiated the assignment of Marilyn Rogers, a seasoned ABC partner with considerable SAP experience, to head up the GMI account. It was agreed that ABC would take the lead on this initial financial systems application with the objective of transferring ABC's SAP R/3 process knowledge and implementation methodology to the GMI team as the project was executed. The first phase of the SAP software conversion was budgeted for fourteen months and $6 million. Cunningham estimated the total cost for the SAP initiative over the five years to follow would be an additional $50 million.

The Financials 2000 project ran smoothly from its start in September 1998. Marilyn Rogers brought with her a well-tested project management process and a set of ABC consultants with recent experience on a nearly identical project. The GMI project team members were hardworking and quick learners. The preliminary draft of the chart-of-accounts hammered out by Linker got the project off to a fast start, and Linker's continued involvement kept it moving.

Within four months the GMI team had completed its basic training in the SAP software and ABC's project management methodology. By February 1999, as part of what we would call the *Build and Test* stage of implementation, it had constructed a conference room prototype of GMI's new financial applications. The prototype was used as a vehicle to refine Linker's design, and weekly meetings were held to discuss and resolve technical design problems as they were encountered. After four weeks of tuning, the software capability was ready for deployment into specific plants and regions. It was at this point that things threatened to bog down.

The Deployment Challenge to Financials 2000
The technical challenges of building the conference room prototype were modest in comparison to the organizational challenge of deploying it into GMI operating locations. To run the accounting modules of R/3 in the integrated manner that Linker was banking on, common data definitions and a standard chart-of-accounts for the entire company had to be adopted and then

codified into R/3 "process tables." Such standards became known as *shared global designs* (SGDs). Ideally a single SGD would be used at all facilities in all business units, and standard software modules from SAP R/3 would support these common procedures. In this case, GMI would enjoy the benefits of shared best practices and the ability to collaborate easily across business units, which were two strategic objectives of GMI-2004. At the same time, Cunningham would avoid the heavy maintenance expense associated with migrating software patches forward if GMI were to later move on to a new release of R/3.

Rarely is the ideal level of integration achieved. Sometimes local customs, government regulations, and market requirements truly preclude common practices, but more often organizational inertia and "not-invented-here" attitudes create obstacles to common practice when none need exist. As a compromise between the ideal SGD set and one that was realistically achievable, Linker had worked with his controllers to create what he called an "80-15-5" design. He strove to define global operating practices with 80 percent commonality that could be supported by standard R/3 modules. Then an additional 15 percent of the practices might be adopted as common regional standards and ideally supported by SAP. The final 5 percent might be locally customized if needed. Although Linker had negotiated such a design with his controllers, the new chart-of-accounts met with immediate resistance at the time of deployment.

Marilyn Rogers had anticipated resistance. She knew that objections would be raised as regional managers began to understand the operational difficulties and expenses associated with the new corporate procedures for data capture, coding, and reconciliation. There was little benefit to be derived locally from the accounting changes and few welcomed the new set of eyes that corporate would soon be able to bring to bear on their operations. Rogers had therefore scheduled a set of project activities that were designed to vent objections and concerns early during deployment. She was unsurprised when people asserted that most of the changes that were about to take place were unnecessary and further that some were unworkable given local operating constraints or legal requirements.

It took weeks to understand all the objections. Some were legitimate and others arose from poor explanations and misunderstandings. Most, however, simply reflected a reluctance on the part of local managers to change what appeared to be working for them. It was clear from these conversations with local management that the GMI-2004 vision of a tightly integrated global corporation had not been uniformly understood, or at least welcomed, everywhere in the company.

Where elements of Linker's financial system design proved to be flawed, adjustments were made. And where local exemptions to the standard policies were necessary, they were granted. But where resistance to the new system was based simply on an unwillingness to change, Linker got tough, involving Brett Berger in the debate. After a highly visible and vocal plant manager was told by Berger to find more suitable employment if he was unwilling to accommodate the changes, resistance at the operating locations subsided. The message was clear—Financials 2000 was for real.

The Importance of Regular Steering Committee Meetings

As the Financials 2000 applications were rolled out across locations in the United States, Europe, and Asia, other unanticipated problems arose. At the insistence of Marilyn Rogers, a weekly Friday steering committee meeting was instituted to deal with problems as soon as they surfaced. Linker, Cunningham, and Rogers seldom missed these meetings. Therefore, team members as well as those affected by the project knew that they had a regular opportunity to raise any issue or objection that they might have.

By addressing concerns as soon as they emerged, Rogers kept them from festering into full-blown problems. The goal of the Friday meetings was to track progress to schedule and to surface problems that might compromise the success of the project. Four questions set the weekly agenda during both the Build and Test and the Capability Deployment stages of implementation:

- Have prerequisite organization and process infrastructure changes been completed?
- Have operating process changes occurred as planned and on schedule?
- Is the workforce appropriately equipped, trained, and motivated to accept these changes?
- Have the planned business capabilities been achieved on schedule? Have they been
  - Tailored to fit local operations and market conditions?
  - Deployed and proven to achieve performance targets?
  - Fully activated and legacy processes removed?
  - Stabilized so that operations can be handed off to line management?

The weekly meetings, which often involved a teleconference with individuals in one or more remote locations, would last until all issues were aired and action plans were formulated to address problems. Progress on problem resolution was then tracked until problems were solved. To the delight of Harry Linker, the process worked effectively and the entire implementation effort moved forward faster than scheduled. Financials 2000 was eventually completed within budget and two months earlier than planned.

More Targets of Opportunity

A second SAP system project called *GMI-Employee Advantage* began under the sponsorship of the Human Resources function in March 1999, six months after the launch of Financials 2000. Using the company's newly constructed intranet, the system allowed employees to access their personnel records and permitted them to coordinate and register for benefits online from office terminals using a standard Web browser. It facilitated access to technical training materials as well as corporate policy and procedure manuals. Finally, in coordination with the accounting group, the system standardized and automated the processes used to make travel arrangements and to submit expense reports throughout the company. The project ran smoothly from start to finish.

A third target of opportunity, *Production Maintenance,* emerged in June 1999. This application supported the activities of planning and performing the critical activities of preventive maintenance and equipment repair within GMI's plants. Using the new software, maintenance activities could be managed and measured; service-parts inventory levels could be established and maintained; and repair completion and expenses could be monitored. The combination of improved availability of service parts, the savings in inventories, and the reduction in equipment downtime was projected to provide a fourteen-month payback on the $2 million investment required to install this software. This project too proved to be a success.

Your Analysis

1. Why were Linker and Cunningham so focused on maintaining common data standards and operating procedures in the form of shared global designs? How achievable do you believe that this objective would be in practice?

2. What factors of success contributed to the fast and steady progress that Financials 2000 made during its implementation?

Assessment of Initial Progress

With adequate journey preparation complete in September 1998, it was possible to begin implementation of the planned business process changes. There were many roads on which the journey might move forward. It was important at the outset to choose the best one and to proceed along it in the right way.

The Importance of Shared Global Designs
Linker and Cunningham were understandably concerned about standardization. SGDs—common data standards and operating procedures—were needed both to control the cost of maintaining the SAP R/3 software and to achieve the organizational synergy that was planned for as a part of GMI-2004. Moreover, since comparable standardization work would be needed to establish shared best practices in marketing, logistics, and manufacturing for the corporation, it was essential that the SAP team establish a workable way to create standard definitions and operating procedures and then form them into SGDs. The goal of a single global standard, predictably enough, proved impossible to achieve because of regional customer requirements and government regulations. Linker's more modest goal of an 80-15-5 design was attainable.

Factors Contributing to Successful
Implementation of Financials 2000
Five factors were important to the success of Financials 2000. First, the objectives of the program were clear—the goal was to replace the hodgepodge of financial applications with the new SAP software and run it on a worldwide basis. Second, there was strong sponsorship from CEO Brett Berger as evidenced by his immediate confrontation of program resistance. Third, the recent comparable experience of the ABC staff, provided by Marilyn Rogers, greatly smoothed the software transfer. Fourth, Harry Linker was actively involved; his continuing pressure on

his regional controllers assured rapid creation and adoption of a shared global design for financial reporting. Fifth, the weekly project reviews that occurred throughout the implementation phase were essential for keeping the project on schedule.

Because of these success factors, Financials 2000 quickly jumped ahead of schedule and was eventually completed within budget and earlier than planned. The success of the project was paralleled by two additional projects which were also well managed: Employee Advantage and Production Maintenance. The thorough planning and journey preparations in 1998 were now paying dividends. As we see them, the years 1998 and 1999 brought nearly flawless execution of Linker's plans.

■ Phase 3 Projects for Business Unit Operations

To complement the three targets of opportunity that arose out of the administrative and support functions within GMI, CIO Cunningham understood the need to gain experience with SAP modules that focused on the marketing, logistics, and manufacturing systems of the business units. It was here that the great bulk of the operating productivity gains would be found. It was also here that the greatest resistance to change could be expected. These processes were more complex in that they were tied to the specific marketing and manufacturing activities of individual business units. A misstep here could visibly affect daily operations as well as revenues. These application areas were also outside Harry Linker's sphere of control.

Moving to the Front Lines (November 1999–January 2000)

To begin building the team's experience with marketing, logistics, and manufacturing modules of SAP R/3, Cunningham encouraged plant managers and business unit heads to consider the software conversion for their operations. He reasoned with them as follows:

"The transition to the SAP software is inevitable and there are advantages to you in moving to it first. Because this is our initial operations project, I will be able to subsidize 30 percent of your project expense out of my corporate development budget; and what's more important, you will be in the best possible position to affect the design of the shared processes that will then be implemented worldwide. By working with us now, you will exert strong influence on the de facto corporate standard for marketing, logistics, and manufacturing processes for those business units that follow."

It was still a tough sell, however, since no business unit wanted to be the test case for such a delicate undertaking. There was sure to be some short-term pain, compensated for only by long-term benefits—most of which would accumulate outside their own business unit.

Targeting Rochester Muffler

Cunningham targeted his strongest selling efforts on Gary Hewitt, president of Rochester Muffler, a $500 million business unit recently acquired from National Motors Incorporated (NMI). In early 1998, NMI had refocused its strategy on the design, assembly, and marketing of automobiles for the global market. Anything not directly connected with that mission was viewed as a distraction. NMI had, as a result, decided to spin off nine captive component suppliers, which (in sixty-plus years of vertical integration) had developed a bloated overhead structure and substantial excess capacity. Rochester Muffler was one of them.

GMI recognized a place in its Automotive division for Rochester as part of a strategy to provide global full-service outsourcing of fuel management and emission control systems for the major automotive original equipment manufacturers (OEMs). The canister technology that Rochester had perfected for its production of catalytic converters would transfer to the fabrication of fuel cells, a future growth segment planned for the GMI's automotive business. GMI intended to link Rochester's

R&D activities with those of the other automotive business units and to market Rochester's ample manufacturing capacity not only to NMI but also to the lucrative automotive aftermarket as well as to other OEMs. It had been more than sixty years since Rochester had actually had to sell any of its production. As a result, Gary Hewitt, formerly VP of marketing for Action Automotive Inc., had been hired from outside GMI to head up Rochester Muffler.

In acquiring Rochester Muffler, GMI had negotiated an attractive price and a commitment by NMI to continue the purchase of mufflers at the current volumes and prices through December 2001. As part of the sales agreement, NMI had also agreed to continue to support Rochester's business operations by running its data processing systems on the NMI corporate mainframe through June 2002 if need be. Nevertheless, because this I/T service was both expensive and inadequate to support Hewitt's new business model, Hewitt wanted to get Rochester off NMI's mainframe as quickly as possible.

However, Hewitt wasn't eager to go along with Cunningham's SAP plans. Having read disaster stories in the business press regarding the expense and complexity of recent ERP conversions, Hewitt was anxious to avoid the experience. Instead of SAP he was hoping to install a simpler information system called QAD, which he had used successfully at Action Automotive and which he believed was more than adequate for Rochester's needs. To install this new system, however, he would have to convince Linker and Berger of his need for a variance from the corporate mandate to move to SAP. And to accomplish this, he knew it would be helpful to have Keith Cunningham on his side.

The Dialogue Between Hewitt and Cunningham
Hewitt put it this way:

"Listen, Keith, I don't want to be the first to move to the SAP platform. We both know that your people will be learning about this new software on the fly, and that it will take longer and cost me more to come up on SAP than it will if I convert to

QAD. Keith, help me out here. Get me up and running on QAD for now and we can migrate over to SAP after a few years if you still think it makes sense.

"If I go onto SAP right now, the other business units are going to sit on the sidelines and watch us flail around. They will see what happens and then negotiate changes to the SGDs and to my processes after I have gone through the pain of installing them. On the other hand, if I can disconnect from the corporate standards, I will have a better chance of getting this thing up and running. It will also give me more freedom to adapt the software quickly to support changes in business processes as my new team and I figure out how to operate successfully in our new market space."

"Gary, I understand where you're coming from on this," Cunningham replied. "Your primary responsibility to the company is to assure the success of Rochester's new business plan and you are reluctant to take on any I/T infrastructure investment activities beyond those required for this immediate goal. I can't force you to use SAP, but I do have an obligation to alert Harry and Brett if you plan to move onto QAD. The three of you will have to work this out." He went on to underscore the downside of Hewitt's proposal: "You do realize of course that if you get the variance that you are asking for and subsequently things go haywire with the QAD software, my I/T staff will not be able to bail you out since they will have had no training or experience with the QAD package."

Hewitt would in effect be committing to running his own data processing operation at the same time he was trying both to streamline his manufacturing operation and to establish a marketing and sales function at Rochester. He did not relish the prospect of being hung out to dry if problems developed with QAD, and he was aware that there had been some "system difficulties" on Action Automotive's previous implementation of the software.

Cunningham also highlighted the impact that the software investment would have on Rochester Muffler's financial performance.

"Given the choice between SAP and QAD, your profitability and RONA performance are going to be noticeably better with SAP. By accounting convention, software project costs are capitalized and written off over a three- to five-year period commencing with the date of successful implementation. You'll see some negative cash flows during the development period, but they won't have any negative impact on accounting profits—project costs are capitalized on the balance sheet but not yet depreciated as an expense in the income statement. Moreover, during this development period the salaries of regular employees participating on the project can be capitalized—which will actually improve your accounting profits at that moment.

"If you participate in the SAP project, you will absorb only your allocated share of its total cost—probably a third or less of the full QAD costs, which you'll have to eat if you go it alone. In addition, if you are truly planning to convert to SAP after only two years, then not only will you have to pay your original fair share of the SAP costs at that point, but you will also have to amortize the entire QAD investment over that brief period."

The specter of an expensive, high-risk undertaking was quite unattractive to Hewitt given everything else that was now on his plate. He was out of options and began thinking seriously of signing up for both the manufacturing and order processing modules of SAP.

Your Analysis

1. What factors affected Cunningham's choice of follow-on projects at the business units?
2. What concerns were raised by Gary Hewitt regarding participation in the project? Were they reasonable?
3. How did Cunningham attempt to alleviate these concerns of line management?

**Assessment of the Move Toward
Logistics and Manufacturing Systems**

In our judgment, as of 1998, Global Systems 2004 team was off
to an excellent start and well positioned to leverage the knowledge, experience, and reputation for success with SAP R/3 that
they had gained during Financials 2000. It was time to apply this
capability to the operational business processes that were to be
converted next.

Factors Affecting the Choice of Follow-On Projects
The principal factor that drove Cunningham's choice of the first
business unit to receive SAP R/3 was the near-certain chance of
success. This was critical both for the morale of his team and for
the professional credibility that would be essential as the R/3
software was subsequently rolled out into other locations. Four
additional factors were also important. First, the project should
be reasonably comprehensive in its use of R/3 modules yet relatively small in scale—a small business unit would do nicely for
this. Second, he wanted a nearly vanilla application of SAP's
current capabilities—with just a few modest modifications so
that the team might gain some experience with the processes
of software modification and its documentation. Third, there
should be some business urgency to force the project forward
quickly. Fourth, the project should have strong commitment and
support from the top of the business unit so that it might progress
as smoothly as had Financials 2000 under the sponsorship of
Harry Linker. With some persuasion aimed at Gary Hewitt,
Rochester Muffler looked like it fit the bill in all respects.

What About Gary Hewitt's Reaction?
Gary Hewitt had some legitimate concerns. He was being asked
to volunteer his business unit as a test site for a new suite of software—one that would remove and replace the central nervous

system his business unit depended on for its continued operations. He had no personal experience with SAP and therefore little confidence in achieving the new capabilities that were promised. Furthermore, there were many industry reports of failures with comparable ERP projects, and Cunningham's staff would be learning about the new software as they worked on his applications. In addition, by agreeing to use SAP, Hewitt would have to comply with the shared global designs that it would establish and thereby give up partial control over the design of his operating processes. These facts in combination argued strongly for the adoption of a more familiar software package and a decentralized approach to satisfying his data processing needs.

Cunningham's Response
It seems clear that Cunningham viewed Rochester Muffler as potentially a loose brick in his carefully crafted I/T architecture. If Hewitt were permitted to opt out of the corporate standards, then other business units were sure to follow. This would have a negative impact on the economies of scale that Cunningham was counting on to justify the SAP investment, and it would have a debilitating effect on the achievement of the business goals established for GMI-2004.

Cunningham did four things to steer Hewitt away from his initial choice. First, he offered to subsidize the SAP investment, and second, he made sure that Hewitt understood the financial performance implications of his choice to reject the corporate standard. Third, he made it clear that Hewitt would have to justify his choice of QAD to Berger and Linker. Finally, he pointed out that if Hewitt's variance were granted, then Hewitt would have to deal with the need for ongoing support for QAD from outside the corporation.

SUMMARY

In this chapter we continued our study of the GMI case through the lens of the Journey Management Model. We picked up the story with the initial task of infrastructure building during the preparation phase of GMI-2004. As CFO Linker considered the sequence in which journey programs and their projects should begin, he realized that GMI's current processes of HR development as well as its infrastructures for management accounting and I/T operations were inadequate to support the proposed operating plan. These would have to be addressed before the planned changes to GMI's business processes could take place.

To develop the required skills and competencies, Linker partnered first with the Human Resources function to design a corporate education program aimed at developing new attitudes and process skills within the management ranks. A series of in-house courses was used both to introduce new business concepts and vocabulary and to provide a forum to surface and address concerns, and thereby lessen organizational resistance. The project worked as planned and the competency component of GMI's organization infrastructure was strengthened in preparation for the coming business transformation.

As his second infrastructure project, Linker planned to replace GMI's financial reporting system so as to increase management's ability to see into and control business unit operations. Before he could do this, however, he saw that he would have to rebuild GMI's I/T capabilities. To document the nature and extent of GMI's problems, Linker commissioned an information technology review. He hired ABC-Consulting to do the study and met Keith Cunningham, whom he subsequently hired as GMI's CIO. Cunningham designed a plan, called Global Systems 2004, to build the I/T infrastructure needed to support GMI-2004. He successfully launched the foundation elements of this plan beginning in January 1998 and quickly established a sound platform upon which the new business processes could be built.

With the required infrastructure in place, the implementation of new business processes could begin. The worldwide effort was scheduled to take six years, beginning in September 1998. It would start in the United States and extend through Europe and Asia, first for support processes and later for marketing, logistics, and manufacturing. SAP R/3 technology was selected as the vehicle for installing the planned changes. Implementation began with SAP's accounting modules in support of Linker's financial reporting project, called Financials 2000.

The Financials 2000 project ran smoothly from the start. ABC-Consulting brought in a well-tested project management process and a set of consultants with recent experience on a nearly identical project. The GMI project team was well chosen and given ample support for the project from its sponsor, CFO Harry Linker. As a result, the Financials 2000 was successfully completed on budget and two months ahead of schedule. This success was soon followed by two additional well-managed projects: Employee Advantage and Production Maintenance.

To complement these three projects addressing administrative and support activities within GMI, Cunningham recognized the need to gain experience with the SAP modules for marketing, logistics, and manufacturing within the business units. It was here that the great bulk of the operating productivity gains would be found. Cunningham focused his marketing attention on Gary Hewitt, president of the Rochester Muffler business unit, persuading him to seriously consider signing up for the manufacturing and order processing modules of SAP.

The Journey Management Model requires a number of specific and pointed questions to be asked at intervals. At the end of this chapter, Exhibits 4.1 and 4.2 provide a ready reference for these questions, extracted mainly from Chapters Three and Four. (One set comes from Chapter Six, to complete the picture.)

Questions for Consideration

1. How does this story of infrastructure building within GMI compare to your own experience? What similarities do you see between your experience and this one? What differences?
2. So far, how successful do you expect the company to be at achieving its goals for GMI-2004?
3. To what extent has this chapter been about information technology? How would the investments that have been made to date by CIO Keith Cunningham be justified within your own firm?

4. As Rochester Muffler president Gary Hewitt considers volunteering for the SAP implementation, what do you think the other business unit presidents are thinking about their own pending conversions?

5. Suppose you were GMI's CEO, Brett Berger. At this point, based on what you've read in the last two chapters, what are you likely to know about the progress being made on GMI-2004? Do you feel that this knowledge is adequate?

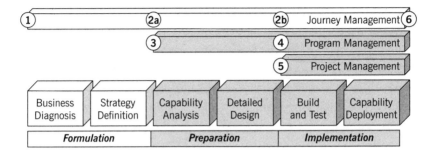

1. Beginning Journey Management
   - Is there an executive management consensus around the need for strategic change?
   - Are influential sponsors for the change program visible and supportive?
   - Has a cross-functional change team been committed to the program, and does this team have the experience, skills, and organizational credibility needed for success?

2. Ongoing Journey Management—Two Iterations
   - Do the journey sponsors remain committed to the strategic vision and business case?
   - Do the facts and assumptions that drive the strategy and its business case remain valid?
   - Are the business capabilities needed to achieve the strategic vision and business case adequately defined?
   - Will the planned infrastructure and process changes deliver these business capabilities?
   - Is the journey broken into manageable programs that deliver these infrastructure and process changes?

3. Beginning Program Management
   - Does line management understand and support the strategic vision and program goals?
   - Is there a common understanding of the new operating plan and its business process implications?
   - Does the business case identify the size and timing of program costs and benefits and create sufficient value to constitute an obvious imperative for the proposed changes?
   - Has a performance plan to measure program achievement against the business case been shared, understood, and accepted, and has it been linked to the compensation and reward system?

Exhibit 4.1. The Timing of Essential Questions for Management.

4. Ongoing Program Management
   - Does management continue to demonstrate active support for the program?
   - Have "quick win" project opportunities been identified and implemented?
   - Have changes in facts and assumptions been reviewed for impact on program plans?
   - Have the strategy, operating plan, and business case been revalidated against changes?
   - Have changes in program scope been documented and appropriately rebudgeted?
   - Have feedback processes been used to manage program budgets and sponsor expectations?

5. Project Management
   - Do clear project specifications define project scope and the time and resources required?
   - Have key employees and needed resources been committed to the project on a sustained basis?
   - Can the project team members articulate the business value that the project will achieve?
   - Is there a specific plan to assess line management against the project objectives and do they understand and accept those objectives?
   - Will the workforce understand and accept the resulting infrastructure and process changes?

6. Concluding Journey Management
   - Have the performance targets been achieved on time and within budget?
   - Are the organization and process infrastructures operating as planned?
   - Have the new business capabilities been achieved as described in the business case?
   - Has an environment been created in which continuous improvement is likely?
   - Are the right measures in place to provide a solid basis for continued value delivery?
   - Is the workforce motivated and rewarded for their contribution and performance?
   - Has management performance been assessed against business case achievement?
   - Are customer needs and expectations being met or exceeded?
   - Are the executive sponsors satisfied with the program results?

Exhibit 4.1. The Timing of Essential Questions for Management, Cont'd.

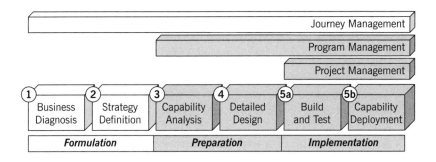

1. Business Diagnosis
   - What is the firm's current strategy for value creation and how well is it working? How do the firm's market position, operating performance, and financial condition compare to those of peers and competitors?
   - What external environment and market dynamics are affecting the organization and its strategy? What market demands, competitive pressures, and regulatory requirements create pressure for change?
   - Is there sufficient documentation of facts for a credible analysis and realistic assessment? Is there a common understanding of these facts and widespread acceptance of the implied need for change?
   - What key strategic alternatives might the organization choose to pursue? What dimensions of company culture or competency can be leveraged moving forward? What aspects of company culture or business environment constrain alternatives? What strategic actions are desirable and which are clearly necessary?

2. Strategy Definition
   - What is the new business vision that motivates the strategic changes that are proposed?
   - What customers, geographies, products, and services are included in the new strategy? What value proposition will differentiate the firm's product and services?
   - What performance measurement plan has been developed to judge progress and to gauge and reward success? What business capabilities are required to achieve these targets and what capability or infrastructure gaps must therefore be addressed?
   - How will technology and people combine with business processes in an operating plan to deliver the planned business capabilities?
   - How will the process changes needed to achieve the operating plan be phased into the organization, and what milestones, checkpoints, and measures will guide the implementation?

Exhibit 4.2. Questions to Address During Journey Stages.

- What is the business case that details and documents the planned costs and benefits and how and when will achievement of the business case be measured?

3. Capability Analysis
   - What specific business process changes will be required to achieve the new operating plan?
   - What process infrastructure changes (information and production) will therefore be required?
   - What organization infrastructure changes (structure, governance, and competence) will be needed?
   - How will the visible measures of performance encourage management and workforce support?

4. Detailed Design
   - Has the program been broken into manageable projects, with appropriate precedence, that achieve measurable goals in a reasonable period?
   - How do program projects combine to deliver the planned infrastructure or business capabilities?
   - Is there an integrated plan to build, test, and deploy each planned capability?
   - Are the roles and responsibilities needed to achieve the capabilities established?
   - Have the key employees and other resources required by the project been identified?
   - Are there project milestones at which to assess progress and the need for adjustments?
   - Do performance metrics motivate desired individual and team-level behavior?

5. Build and Test; Capability Deployment
   - Have prerequisite organization and process infrastructure changes been completed?
   - Have operating process changes occurred as planned and on schedule?
   - Is the workforce appropriately equipped, trained, and motivated to accept these changes?
   - Have the planned business capabilities been achieved on schedule and been
     - Tailored to fit local operations and market conditions?
     - Deployed and proven to achieve performance targets?
     - Fully activated and legacy processes removed?
     - Stabilized so that operations can be handed off to line management?

Exhibit 4.2. Questions to Address During Journey Stages, Cont'd.

5

Reacting to
Abrupt Changes
in Strategic Priorities

n this chapter we pick up the GMI-2004 story in September 1999 as the rollout of Financials 2000 was nearing completion, two months ahead of schedule. Having had strong support and the active participation of CFO Harry Linker, the financial system conversion had moved forward faster than planned. With everything coming together quicker than expected, CFO Harry Linker was feeling confident about the quality of the SAP software and the effectiveness of ABC-Consulting's design tools and project management methodology. It appeared that the subsequent system conversions also might be faster and easier than originally forecast. Everyone associated with the program was optimistic.

■ The Rise of the ACCESS-2002 Program

Unfortunately, new business pressures were beginning to develop. CIO Keith Cunningham quickly found himself compelled to abandon his current implementation plans for Global Systems 2004 in favor of a more aggressive and perilous shortcut aimed at bringing critical SAP modules online two years faster than originally planned.

Gathering Clouds (September 1999–November 1999)

In late September 1999, just as the Global Systems 2004 program was about to deploy operational systems into GMI's divisions in a comprehensive way, GMI ran into strong, unexpected pressure to pick up the pace of implementation. Major Automotive customers had begun to demand online access to GMI's sales, manufacturing, and logistics systems and they were unwilling to wait until 2004 for the ongoing SAP implementation to be completed. This customer requirement triggered a supplemental I/T budget request for $4.9 million to retrofit GMI's legacy information systems for Internet access by December 2001. The GMI board, naturally enough, questioned spending such a large sum on a system that would be abandoned as soon as the SAP implementation was complete.

Such high-level attention directed at the SAP conversion proved to be a good-news–bad-news story for CIO Cunningham. The good news was that the board of directors was about to begin actively tracking the progress of the SAP R/3 rollout and therefore business unit heads no longer needed encouragement to move forward onto the ERP platform. The bad news was that the final phases of the Global Systems 2004 program would be launched almost immediately, nearly a full year sooner than scheduled. Even more problematically, the pace of the rollout was to be twice as fast as originally planned. Although Cunningham's SAP conversion team was not yet adequately prepared for this large an effort, the moment for program launch had arrived. Cunningham had to acquire additional resources quickly and then scramble to achieve the accelerated schedule for the conversion, now called *ACCESS-2002*.

Reasons Behind the Speedup

There was good reason to speed the pace of the SAP rollout. GMI's three biggest customers were large automotive manufacturers. And all three had just committed to participate in AUTOLINK, a new Internet consortium of automotive manufacturers and their suppliers. The goal of AUTOLINK was to force all supply-chain communication henceforth to take place over the Internet, replacing the hodgepodge of phone, fax, and EDI messages through which the system currently operated.

The impact of AUTOLINK on automotive suppliers like GMI could be very serious indeed. The manufacturers wanted Internet handling of all business transactions, as well as the ability to track and control orders and to view supplier inventory and capacity levels. Additionally, their plans envisioned Internet visibility through each tier-1 supplier's manufacturing processes and into its tier-2 suppliers. From all of this it was hoped that current materials cost would be driven down by 10–20 percent. When AUTOLINK was fully implemented, some $275 billion worth of procurement activity was expected to flow across the system each year, so the potential savings were enormous. The plan was to go live with a new system that reached all tier-1 suppliers—including GMI—by January 2002. None of this would be possible with GMI's current business systems— although it would be supported by the new SAP software that was about to be installed.

Responses by Cunningham, Berger, and the Board

Meanwhile, Keith Cunningham had been working proactively on the issue. Anticipating the general nature of the AUTOLINK announcement, Cunningham had studied "the Internet requirement" and believed that it was well in hand. On the basis of a credible analysis performed by an internal I/T task force, he had reported that the legacy software for all mission-critical systems could be made Internet accessible within twenty-four months, that is, by December 2001. This analysis included those I/T infrastructure changes necessary to Internet-enable the existing GMI systems, although it did not envision the richer data-sharing concepts behind the most recent announcement of AUTOLINK. Those additional capabilities could be achieved when the manufacturing and logistics modules of SAP R/3 were fully installed throughout GMI by January 2004. And Cunningham did not believe that the manufacturers would actually be ready for those additional capabilities before that time.

To meet the Internet challenge, Cunningham prepared an I/T capital appropriation request of $4.9 million to contract with an outside vendor, Spartan Systems Inc., for the legacy conversion effort that would meet the needs of AUTOLINK. Brett Berger learned of the proposal and of the urgent need to support AUTOLINK three weeks in advance of the board meeting at which the capital request was to be considered. In view of the size of the request and the customers involved, Berger engaged the accounting firm of Able & Gallo (A&G) to make an independent assessment of GMI's readiness for the AUTOLINK initiative. He postponed the board decision on Cunningham's request, pending A&G's assessment of both Cunningham's plan and GMI's overall readiness for the Internet.

Advice from Able & Gallo

A&G's conclusions were alarming. The accountants' report expressed "grave concerns" over what they considered

- An ambitious schedule of reprogramming and unit testing for the nearly five hundred applications that had been identified as needing Internet conversion.
- The potentials for subtle interdependencies between applications that were scheduled for Internet conversion and four hundred others that were to be left unchanged.
- The lack of a formal, integrated testing procedure at the end of the scheduled conversion process in December 2001.
- The heavy reliance upon Spartan Systems, a relatively small software consulting company made up largely of independent contract programmers.

If the proposed plan were to fail, A&G argued, at least some of GMI's customers would seek other suppliers, and those who remained would expect lower prices and faster delivery than would be possible for GMI to deliver. This was a risk that they believed that GMI management could not find acceptable. They recommended choosing one of these courses of action:

An in-depth analysis and remediation of all "legacy applications" and an integrated test of all modified business applications by August 2001 at the latest. This extra scope and faster pace of work would require the replacement (or augmentation) of the proposed vendor, Spartan Systems, and was projected to increase the cost of the proposal from Cunningham's $4.9 million to $7.6 million.

or

The replacement of all existing legacy applications with new software modules that would provide the necessary Internet connectivity and "see through" capability. The SAP software that Cunningham had planned to roll out over a four-year period would satisfy this requirement if it could be installed during the next two years.

This choice triggered two reasonable questions by the board: "Why would we spend $7.6 million or even $4.9 million to update current applications if we were planning to retire them all in a matter of a year or two? Why can't we speed up the SAP R/3 implementation and thereby kill two birds with one stone?"

Cunningham knew that the board would not be satisfied by arguments such as "willing partners in process change," "manageable pace of implementation," and "lower consulting expenses." Each response had a viable counterargument. First, the board believed that CEO Berger could demand cooperation from the business unit heads and thereby assure their willingness to work with Cunningham to accomplish whatever needed to be done. Second, as a part of A&G's own Change Management practice, A&G assisted clients in managing changes of the kind entailed by an ERP implementation. As a competitor to ABC-Consulting, A&G had significant expertise with the SAP R/3 product; and its management had already offered their experience, methodologies, and assistance in managing the new ACCESS-2002 program.

Finally, Cunningham would face the argument that the additional expense of contracting out the bulk of the SAP conversion work ($56 million on top of Cunningham's original estimate of $50 million) would be more than offset by an earlier realization of the benefit stream from the GMI-2004. Based on a study of industry benchmarks and what they considered a conservative extrapolation from best practices, A&G staff estimated that an annual benefit of $40 to $70 million could be achieved from a redesign of GMI business processes. These programmed savings, summarized in Figure 5.1, would arise in four categories: centralization of purchasing, elimination of redundant tasks, automation of clerical processes, and reduction of supervisory staff by providing the workforce better access to information and decision-making tools. The A&G analysis showed, for example, that GMI's best competitor had revenues per employee that were 25 percent higher.

Activity	Savings
Centralize Purchasing • Reduced headcount • Improved pricing • Reduced inventory	$1–2 million $6–8 million $10–16 million
Eliminate Work • Faster work flows • Increased productivity	$1–2 million $4–8 million
Automate Processes • Reduced operating expenses • Increased productivity	$8–15 million $6–10 million
Informate Workforce • Reduced supervision	$6–12 million
Total	**>$40 Million**

Figure 5.1. A&G Estimate of Annual Benefits from ACCESS-2002.

Therefore, comparable performance at GMI would eliminate the need for 20 percent of the current workforce. And thus if the goals of GMI-2004 could be achieved two years earlier through the rapid implementation of ACCESS-2002, then the A&G business case was compelling.

Cunningham attempted to urge caution against the accelerated schedule, but Berger and Linker ignored his advice. He then proposed what he called "Plan B," which was to proceed in parallel with the $4.9 million remediation of the legacy system even as GMI moved forward with the accelerated ACCESS-2002 implementation schedule. "Plan B" would offer a fallback position for the company in the event that the new, aggressive schedule could not be achieved. The incremental $4.9 million expense could be viewed as insurance to protect the business from the possibility of a catastrophic failure.

Considering the recent success of Financials 2000, Berger dismissed this fallback plan as frivolous. The board was growing impatient to see the performance improvements that had been promised three years ago as part of the GMI-2004 restructuring. Besides, current operating profits and free cash flow were noticeably below forecast. "It's time to just do it," he said.

The Decision to Begin ACCESS-2002
Momentum grew and a consensus emerged to step up the planned SAP conversion schedule. With the concurrence of the board, Berger soon gave direction to begin the acceleration with six stringent conditions on schedule, cost, and outcomes for the new program. GMI management would be expected to

- Use the ACCESS-2002 program as an opportunity to reengineer existing business processes.
- Adopt the best practices of SAP, wherever practical, in the definition of new business processes.
- Use a single shared global design (SGD) for business processes, wherever possible, in keeping with the strategy of operating as a global company.
- Collaborate across business units and allocate sufficient internal resources to ensure the success of the ACCESS-2002 program.
- Complete ACCESS-2002 by December 1, 2001, tightly managing its budget of $106 million.
- Harvest sufficient operating benefits from the new integrated business system to justify its installation.

Cunningham watched uncomfortably as a memo describing ACCESS-2002 and directing the forced march was prepared. Whether he liked it or not, the band was tuning up and he needed to get out in front if he were to have any hope of leading the parade.

Because of the new end date for the SAP rollout as part of ACCESS-2002, Cunningham's first order of business was to revisit the preparations he had made for SAP implementation as part of

Global Systems 2004. The rollout's deliverables would have to be reestablished, and then the schedule of required projects and their needed resources would have to be recalculated. Clearly, additional help was now needed from outside the firm and, depending on the bidding process, a new consulting firm might be hired. Also, since the end date for ACCESS-2002 was set for December 1, 2001, and its budget was fixed at $106 million, the scope of the program would have to be adjusted to fit within those constraints.

The Response of ABC-Consulting
One thing was for sure, Keith Cunningham did not want to switch consulting firms from ABC to A&G. First, there had been some tension between himself and the A&G team that had reviewed his Internet proposal. More important, GMI had invested too much time and intellectual capital in the existing relationship with ABC and its development methodology. Linker, who had become a fan of ABC as a result of his success with the Financials 2000 implementation, agreed. The current team was working well together and had won the respect of key managers within the business units as a result of that project.

Cunningham and Linker met with Marilyn Rogers, the ABC-Consulting partner, to explain the recent developments and to discuss the A&G plan to accelerate the Global Systems 2004 implementation schedule. Upon hearing the news, Rogers was incredulous.

"No way! No damn way are you going to achieve the Global Systems 2004 objectives in the next twenty-four months. What you are hoping to accomplish will realistically take us the next four years. At best you could do it in three if everything was to go right as it did with Financials 2000."

"Listen, Marilyn," Linker replied, "A&G has convinced Brett that they can do this job and the board has said that they want it done. GMI is going forward with the plan with you or without you. As I see it you have two options: either you are going to finish your current projects, pick up your check, and forget about the remaining $48 million in work that we have implicitly agreed would be yours over the next four years, or you are going to make a competitive bid on the $106 million engagement that A&G has proposed to do for us over the next twenty-four months."

"Harry," Marilyn countered, "what they are proposing to do is slam in the SAP software, not facilitate the organizational changes that you have told me that you want to accomplish. If you just want Internet software running on your hardware and you don't care how it operates, then I can remove the shrink-wrap and shove it into all of your facilities as well as they can. I could do that in twenty-four months. Hell, I could do *that* in twelve months with the $106 million they are asking for. When the smoke clears, however, you won't be happy. What comes out of the box will not support the way you operate today. And it surely won't support the way you want to operate in the future. If you were to tell me that you wanted all of the SAP modules running effectively in two or three of your business units, I could bring on additional staff and we could do that for you in twenty-four months. But all data processing and process changes in all business units in both divisions in twenty-four months—no way!

"Just look at their schedule," she continued. "They have allocated three weeks to design the SGD for the manufacturing module. We had been planning on three months and that was optimistic. You remember the trouble we had getting the business unit controllers to agree on the financial SGD and the common chart-of-accounts. And Harry, those were your guys—they reported to you; you had some leverage on them. Think about the stubborn personalities in manufacturing. It is going to take time for them to get over the shock that their processes are really going to change. It will then take time to document their current procedures to understand their strengths and weaknesses, their commonalties and their differences. We will then need to find some common ground between existing practices and to negotiate a compromise collection of practices that everyone can live with. If we were given only three weeks, the best we could do would be to replicate what we are now doing in each of the factories. It will take more than three weeks to formulate a new shared vision and to build consensus around it."

"Calm down, Marilyn!" said Linker. "I am not the enemy. I do understand what you are saying. I am not looking for the 100 percent solution here. There is pressure on Brett to deliver on some of the operational improvements that he has promised the board, and it can't wait four years. We have to go after some low-hanging fruit right now and he is prepared to spend what it takes to get it. If we can get even 60 percent of the benefits with 20 percent of the reengineering and consensus work that you have budgeted for, then I will be satisfied. There is lots of opportunity in these operations. Let's think of it as going through the first time fast and picking what is obvious and easy; and then if it makes sense we can go back through again after the system is up and running to pick up what we missed. Set your implementation schedule assuming that we will get rapid agreement on the new process designs. If we reach an impasse, I guarantee you that we will get you a decision on any process design issue within forty-eight hours of your request.

"I've talked to Berger about this and he is in agreement," Linker continued. "We are realistic about what we are asking you to do and we understand the difficulty of what lies ahead both for your people and for ours. But we see no reasonable alternative to accelerating the current plan. So I am telling you, if you can take care of the project management dimension of this, we can take care of getting you the cooperation that you are going to need from the business units. Berger even offered to get personally involved with this. He said that if we need his help, we can call on him at any time."

Marilyn Rogers looked directly at Linker and repeated what she had just heard: "You will get me consensus on the process designs. All impasses will be resolved within two days. GMI is willing to forgo 40 percent of the original program benefits. Berger is aware of this and we have access to him if we need it. Did I hear you correctly, Harry?"

"Right! Indeed you did," said Linker. "You manage the program to the schedule we have set, and Berger and I will get the organization aligned behind you."

Marilyn Rogers made eye contact with Cunningham to make sure that he had been listening. She wanted to emphasize the agreement that had just been established. Given specifications for the business processes and the more modest objectives that they seemed willing to accept, she knew that she could deliver the system in twenty-four months. She was now off the hook, and the monkey would be on Linker's back to force consensus on the process designs. It was possible that he could repeat what he had just done with Financials 2000. If Rogers had learned anything from her ERP project experiences over the past nine years, it was that *anything* was possible on an ERP engagement.

Marilyn was feeling an adrenaline high as the meeting adjourned. She clearly had the inside track on a major piece of work that had fallen into her lap unexpectedly as she was about to enter the final quarter of 1999. She had walked into the meeting believing that she might lose the $48 million worth of business that she had budgeted for at GMI over the next four years. But now instead, the account was likely to jump from $12 million to $53 million in each of the next two years. The additional work could double her bonus for the current year and the next two as well. And while the implementation work would be intense for all involved with this new ACCESS-2002 program, she was confident that she could deliver as promised—provided that Linker could hold up his part of the bargain.

Rogers knew she had to summarize the day's discussion in a memo of understanding as part of the proposal that she and her staff would now prepare. Linker's directive to focus on the "low-hanging fruit" implied that only those processes that either offered a very large payoff or could be implemented with minimal effort would be addressed during the next twenty-four months. Many process-reengineering opportunities would have to be bypassed to achieve the new December 2001 deadline. Negotiations between Rogers, Linker, and Cunningham during November 1999 led to an agreement as to which SAP modules were to be in and out of scope of work for ACCESS-2002. Figure 5.2 summarizes this agreement. Although the revised program scope was documented by ABC-Consulting in a letter of understanding, the compromises in program benefits were not reflected in a revised business case by Harry Linker, nor were they ever explicitly communicated to Brett Berger and the board.

Your Analysis

1. In your experience, how likely is it that so dramatic a change of direction would be imposed on an ongoing program of strategic change?
2. What were the reactions of the actors in this story to accelerating the SAP implementation? Are any going off track in the GMI-2004 journey? Which ones? How so? In what respects are they departing from the Journey Management Model?

Assessment of the Change in Direction

The implementation problems that occur during a journey of strategic change often stem from failure to recognize and appropriately respond to shifts in strategic context. Both vigilance for signs of such context shifts and willingness to adapt implementation plans quickly are critical to maintaining management

	Previously Completed	Access 2002	Out of Scope	Business Process
Finance and Accounting	X			Accounts receivable and payable
	X			Asset accounting
		X		Cash management and forecasting
	X			Cost-element and cost-center accounting
			X	Executive information system
	X			Financial consolidation
	X			General ledger
			X	Product-cost accounting
			X	Profitability analysis
	X			Profit-center accounting
		X		Standard and period-related costing
Logistics and Manufacturing		X		Inventory management
		X		Material requirements planning
		X		Materials management
	X			Plant maintenance
		X		Production planning
			X	Project management
		X		Purchasing
			X	Quality management
			X	Routing management
		X		Shipment tracking
			X	Vendor evaluation
Human Resources		X		Human-resources time accounting
			X	Payroll
			X	Personnel planning
	X			Travel expenses
	X			Employee benefits
Sales and Marketing		X		Order entry and management
			X	Pricing and customer profitability
			X	Customer relationship management
		X		Sales planning
			X	Credit management
		X		Available-to-promise

Figure 5.2. SAP Modules in the Scope of Work for ACCESS-2002.

control over a strategic journey. In addition, the adjustment of the current business case is essential to managing sponsor expectations and to setting priorities for implementation.

Likelihood of Dramatic Shifts in Direction
In today's dynamic world of business, shifts in the strategic context of a firm are commonplace. A reality and a challenge of transformational changes within large corporations is that they take a long time. So long, in fact, that the conditions and assumptions upon which the goals of the journey were established often change. In the case of GMI, new strategic plans of key customers created an immediate need for online access to operating data. This required adaptation of GMI's current manufacturing and logistics processes, which in turn required changes to the existing I/T systems. A hazardous, two-year acceleration of the ongoing SAP implementation was the result. While this specific shift in strategic context could not have been foreseen at the start of the journey in 1998, it should have been handled differently once it occurred.

Reaction to the Change in Customer Requirements
Cunningham's proposal to handle the new AUTOLINK requirements outside the ongoing Global Systems 2004 program made sense from his perspective. He was confident that he could deliver on the objectives of the current program if he had the chance to roll it out as scheduled. However, he feared the collapse of that program if it were accelerated to outstrip his resources. Thus, rather than disrupt what was now going well, he proposed to spend an additional $4.9 million on software modifications to the legacy systems.

Brett Berger naturally found the idea of spending $4.9 million more on software maintenance unattractive. GMI's profits for 1998 were once again below forecast and the board was anxious to see the fruits of the large investment that it had been making in GMI-2004. Berger viewed the new customer requirements as an opportunity to force forward the benefits promised by GMI-2004. Believing that it was time for bold action, Berger found it reasonable to challenge Cunningham's cautious plan. When an independent review of the situation confirmed that an acceleration of the I/T program was possible, the conclusion was obvious—advance the schedule.

Harry Linker supported the decision. Given the pressure that Berger was feeling from the board to show performance improvements soon, he understood that there was no political alternative to accelerated implementation. Buoyed by the success of Financials 2000 project and confident in the project management process and skills that had recently developed within GMI, he too pressed Cunningham to move forward. In the process, Linker either underestimated the importance of his power over his controllers to his success with Financials 2000 or overestimated the control he could exert over his peers and their direct reports as he moved forward with ACCESS-2002, or both.

Although Linker recognized the need to renegotiate program scope with Marilyn Rogers, he chose not to revisit the GMI-2004 business case that had been developed earlier, even though this business case contained the original justification for the Global Systems 2004 program. Daunted by the time and energy that it would require, and wanting to avoid the new round of organizational objections that it would unleash, Linker decided not to document the impact of the new program scope on the planned GMI-2004 business benefits. It did seem likely that even the reduced implementation benefits would be more than adequate to justify the ACCESS-2002 program. For whatever reason, he did not share this thinking with Berger and the board, nor did he explicitly inform them of the change of program scope.

Marilyn Rogers obviously did not want to lose the GMI account and would do whatever she could within reason to retain the business. The A&G proposal to accelerate Global Systems 2004 had already been embraced by Brett Berger and supported by Harry Linker. Her protests to Linker were strong but ineffective. She pointed out the risks of a hasty implementation and observed that the business benefits originally planned could not be achieved in the new time frame. Linker understood—yet planned to proceed in any event. He made it clear that A&G was prepared to step forward and execute a program if ABC-Consulting could not. She was given an ultimatum to either sign up or ship out.

Thus the GMI engagement that Rogers had planned for the next four years had been terminated. Her customer had changed his mind. He now had a new need and was requesting a proposal. She had little choice but to offer one—which was eventually accepted. Wisely, her first step before agreeing to participate in ACCESS-2002 was to nail down specifically which core business processes—purchasing, customer order processing, and inventory management—would be redesigned and standardized across all business units and which would be either replicated as is or totally bypassed. She was undoubtedly looking two years forward to the post-implementation assessment that would surely occur, and preparing for the inevitable question: Have you delivered everything that was contracted for? One might fault Rogers at this point for not forcing an explicit definition of business benefits to be gained from the investment. She should have known that this would be important to Berger eventually. There again, she could rationalize that she had given good advice to a client who had simply chosen to ignore it. In any event, bypassing Linker to talk directly to Berger would probably have cost her the account.

Keith Cunningham now stood at a critical crossroads. His well-laid plans for Global Systems 2004 had been derailed and his advice to invest in a backup plan had been rejected. He now faced a tough choice. Should he go along with an implementation plan that he knew had a substantial chance of ending in disappointment? Or should he place his job at risk by refusing to support the plan? This dilemma was exacerbated by the fact that he had little basis, other than professional intuition, upon which to build a strong argument.

This is where our Journey Management Model shows its strength. Had GMI management bought into the model and followed it here, Cunningham would have had a process to review the potential problems in a natural way. Specifically, the decision to accelerate the implementation schedule would be a clear trigger for the management team to return to questions of both journey and program management and thus to review the facts and assumptions that were driving the current work. The analysis would show that the business case on which the original GMI-2004 journey was sold was no longer valid. In the discussions that followed, it might have been agreed that there was no political alternative but to move forward with ACCESS-2002. And further it might have proven true, as Linker believed, that the new, more limited objectives of ACCESS-2002 were still sufficient to financially justify its implementation. But neither justification was documented, and as launched the program was set up to disappoint executive management at its conclusion.

Admittedly, it can be time-consuming, expensive, and sometimes painful to monitor ongoing events and to reassess the working assumptions and the business case for a journey in light of key changes. Nevertheless, this work is absolutely essential during an extended journey such as GMI-2004. As outlined in Chapter Four, one must regularly ask these Journey Management questions:

- Do the journey sponsors remain committed to the strategic vision and business case?
- Do the facts and assumptions that drive the strategy and its business case remain valid?

- Are the business capabilities needed to achieve the strategic vision and business case adequately defined?
- Will the planned infrastructure and process changes deliver the planned business capabilities?
- Is the journey broken into manageable programs that deliver these infrastructure and process changes?

And at the level of Program Management one must continually ask these questions:

- Does management continue to demonstrate active support for the program?
- Have "quick win" project opportunities been identified and implemented?
- Have changes in facts and assumptions been reviewed for impact on program plans?
- Have the strategy, operating plan, and business case been revalidated against changes?
- Have changes in program scope been documented and appropriately rebudgeted?
- Have feedback processes been used to manage program budgets and sponsor expectations?

The answers to many of these questions for GMI-2004 were now uncertain in light of the decision to narrow the scope of the work. By pursuing the issues raised by these questions, Cunningham would have had the opportunity to define criteria of success for ACCESS-2002. These criteria could then guide both program execution and a post-implementation assessment.

In summary, what had begun in January 1998 as a series of I/T infrastructure investments that were clearly designed to support a new business strategy had now taken on a new purpose. The recent negotiations between Harry Linker and ABC-Consulting had not been about business performance objectives,

they'd been about which SAP modules were in and out of scope
for ACCESS-2002. The program had become "a construction
project" driven by a fixed budget and an immovable end date.
In the months ahead the program scope would further contract
on several occasions to accommodate these constraints. Because
there was now no linkage to the GMI-2004 business case, the
program had been cut loose from its attachment to strategic
business objectives.

■ Implementation of ACCESS-2002

By late November 1999, the decision to launch an accelerated ERP
initiative had been reached and the scope of work for the new
program, ACCESS-2002, had been negotiated among Marilyn
Rogers, Harry Linker, and Keith Cunningham. It was now time
to implement the plan.

Setting the New Course (December 1999–September 2000)

The ACCESS-2002 program was announced with much fanfare
at corporate headquarters, then quickly divided along two paths
with differing levels of management support and perceived urgency. The Automotive division strongly embraced it—especially the staff of Rochester Muffler, for whom it provided the
AUTOLINK Internet interface they needed to keep their key customers and simultaneously offered an escape from the very expensive I/T services currently being supplied by their old parent
company, NMI.

In the Industrial division, however, the program was
viewed as unnecessary and unwelcome corporate meddling in
local business practices. People quickly saw that although SAP
conversion might simplify financial consolidations at corporate
headquarters, it would disrupt ongoing operations in the busi-

ness units, create a new depreciation expense for the division, and return little or nothing to the business in way of operating benefits.

The ACCESS-2002 Announcement and Response
A newsletter describing the scope and purpose of ACCESS-2002 was sent to all GMI employees on December 1, 1999. It announced that as part of a strategic conversion to online customer relationships, the corporation was preparing to standardize the information systems of all business units by installing SAP R/3 software at all operating locations. It highlighted the critical nature of the program schedule created by the deadline for real-time Internet access set by their primary customers. (That date had moved two months closer as the decision to accelerate the SAP implementation was debated, the terms of the new consulting contract were established, and ABC-Consulting was eventually selected as the vendor of choice.) The newsletter announcing ACCESS-2002 further explained that the new system was an essential platform for strategic operating changes that had been planned for the years ahead. ACCESS-2002 was hailed as a new beginning in the history of the corporation. Not only would it enable GMI to better serve its customers globally, it would also reduce inventory by opening Internet connections with suppliers, enhance management decision making, achieve significant economies of scale, and possibly create a sustainable competitive advantage over the company's rivals. ACCESS-2002 was clearly established as a strategic imperative, to be driven forward under a firm delivery deadline of December 1, 2001. The program was to begin within Rochester Muffler, first in the United States and then in Europe. It would then spread simultaneously through the remainder of the Automotive division and into the Industrial division.

The news was received with enthusiasm by many. For some business unit managers the backlog of I/T application change requests had been a long-standing source of frustration; they viewed their information systems as the key obstacle to many important process changes that they knew were needed in their operations. In addition, John Nolte (corporate VP-Manufacturing) liked the idea that the process standardization required by SAP R/3 would cause the wide variety of manufacturing processes in GMI's twenty-seven plants to be analyzed and compared. Prior attempts to gain consensus on common practices had been thwarted by sharp divisional and regional rivalries. ACCESS-2002 offered hope of a set of best practices that could be shared across all plants.

Beginning Implementation in the Automotive Division
The key to the high-speed rollout planned for ACCESS-2002 was a phased and parallel implementation schedule. The program was broken into projects by function and business unit. The work would commence immediately within the Automotive division at Rochester Muffler, but would proceed at a controlled pace—first in the United States and then in Europe. As the lead site, Rochester Muffler would become the gathering point for the much larger implementation team that was now needed, and Rochester would provide the forum for the team's orientation, education, and training. In addition, the Rochester implementation would produce the shared global designs for use in subsequent deployments. Once the new staff was on board and up to speed and the process design templates were locked in, the program could then cascade quickly across the remainder of the business units. At least that was the plan.

The work of implementation began at Rochester Muffler in early December 1999 with a whirlwind of activity. Its president, Gary Hewitt, subsequently recalled the events of that period for a colleague who was about to begin a comparable process:

> Suddenly all hell broke loose. The ACCESS-2002 program was launched and we were first up. I was drafted as a member of

the ACCESS-2002 executive steering committee and we were expected to meet every Friday from noon until we were done with a detailed project review. Dozens of new faces arrived on site and were roaming through the hallways interviewing my people and collecting and tabulating reams of operating data. Many of my best folks were yanked out of their jobs and assigned full time to the project; we had to hustle to backfill the vacuum that this created. To top this all off, we were in the midst of preparations for the year-end closing.

There were continuous communications back into the organization where people were understandably nervous about all the changes that were imminent. There were meetings on top of meetings: kickoff meetings, planning meetings, process-mapping meetings, reengineering meetings, project review meetings, and informational meetings. In addition, we had a raft of training classes, a telephone hot line, and a weekly newsletter. All were designed to build concepts and a common vocabulary within the organization and to keep everyone up to date as to what was happening.

Some folks were suffering from information overload. It was impossible to participate in all of this and still get all of your regular work done. There was plenty of unpaid overtime worked during that holiday season, but spirits ran high. There was clearly a structure to all of the ongoing activity and nobody had to ask, "Why are we doing this?" We knew we were in a war, but it felt like we were winning it.

Despite the heavy workload, I was actually quite relieved. I had known for nearly a year that we had to get off of the NMI systems sometime before January 2002. But I couldn't get myself to move on it. I guess I was in denial. My last I/T project experience had seemed like a random sequence of unplanned events that was punctuated by a series of missed milestones and business crises. This time it was different. Marilyn Rogers was guiding the entire effort with an incredibly detailed implementation schedule. Every project activity was carefully orchestrated and it was clear to everyone that Berger and the board were watching our progress. There were mandatory classes in teamwork, problem solving, and project management. We were reminded of how to talk to one another—how to disagree without being disagreeable and how to listen to criticism without becoming defensive. Meetings had agendas; people showed up on time; decisions were made; and work products were documented.

The Importance of the Weekly Steering Committee Meeting

The regular steering committee meetings, which had so helped Linker with the success of Financials 2000, became an integral part of ACCESS-2002 at Rochester Muffler. Weekly meetings involving Gary Hewitt, Keith Cunningham, Marilyn Rogers, and the various project team leaders were held each Friday afternoon. The goal of those meetings was to monitor program progress against schedule. They monitored the following points:

- Budgeted resources were committed and deployed as planned.
- Team members were competent and meeting performance expectations.
- Communications and teamwork were working well.
- Buy-in from line management and the workforce was still strong.
- Project management processes were operating effectively.

At these gatherings program team members would have a regular and natural opportunity to meet with the steering committee. Here they could discuss potential problems and obtain clarification and guidance from the committee as needed. Emerging problems thus could be addressed quickly before they had an opportunity to fester.

Marilyn Rogers in particular used these review meetings to move forward the work of establishing shared global designs for GMI. Selection of these SGDs was by far the most controversial of the journey design issues. Decisions made here would not only change business processes and employee jobs and responsibilities, they could also affect the business unit's relationships with customers and suppliers. Reaching a consensus among multiple operating groups across both divisions as to what the new standards should be was a difficult task. Especially when standards were viewed as corporate bureaucracy, the SGD working groups tended to drag their feet. To keep the ACCESS-2002 program on schedule to meet the AUTOLINK deadline, Marilyn Rogers would place troublesome SGD decisions on the steering committee agenda and there attempt to force a choice. If the impasse could not be broken, she would turn finally to Harry Linker to arbitrate a decision. The process was contentious but working adequately.

Some Concern at Rochester Muffler

Gary Hewitt came to appreciate the professionalism with which Marilyn Rogers had organized the ACCESS-2002 program and the skill with which she was able to manage difficult politics while keeping projects on schedule. Nevertheless, as discussed with John Nolte (VP-Manufacturing), Hewitt worried that the shared global design teams might be moving forward too quickly:

> When process design choices need to be made, the ABC staff lays out the alternatives and forces us to pick one. There have been times when I wished that they had been more directive in guiding our selection. We were picking between options in our new marketing and sales system, for example, without understanding what we were committing to. When we tried to defer our decisions to ABC, Rogers threw it right back to us, saying, "You are about to have some really serious plastic surgery here, guys, and I want you to look better than you did before we started. Beauty is in the eye of the beholder and it is only you who can determine how you want to look and perform when we are done."

Of course she was right in some sense, but I still felt cheated. To have confidence in our choices, we need advice on how we might run our business operations. For whatever reason, we haven't been getting it from ABC. It is obvious that the program is moving forward on schedule, but I have the nagging feeling that we might be moving forward in the wrong direction.

Bigger Problems in the Industrial Division

Through August 2000, the Automotive initiative was progressing according to schedule, but there were signs that trouble was brewing in the Industrial division. Management here was openly resisting the implementation and the divisional president, Ralph Lehman, was balking at his new higher expense allocation for the SAP program.

The costs associated with ACCESS-2002 were to be split equally between GMI's two operating divisions. This meant that half of that investment would be capitalized on Industrial's balance sheet and then depreciated over five years once the program was completed. Because of the new accelerated deployment schedule and the increased reliance on outside consultants, the projected capitalization cost was twice as high as the initial estimate for Global Systems 2004, and the depreciation expense would come on stream two years sooner than originally projected. The business unit presidents were to be given no relief in their RONA objectives and thus would be hard-pressed to make their numbers in subsequent years. In addition, Industrial's management was not convinced of the value of standardizing its business processes with those of Automotive, and Industrial's division controller (Bob Halliday) was still questioning whether the idea of shared global designs was feasible. Some new arrivals to Industrial's management team were even challenging the choice of SAP as the software platform and lobbying to have the ERP selection team reconstituted.

In light of its cost concerns, Industrial's management challenged the arrival of every new ABC analyst and balked on the commitment of its most qualified staff to the ACCESS-2002 program. With downsizing efforts ongoing within the division, dozens of short-term employees were available for a final assignment. To reduce program expenses, controller Halliday pushed to substitute these individuals for ABC staff whenever possible. He insisted, for example, that the division could perform its own education and training activities throughout the program. In addition, short-term individuals often found their way into key project meetings as substitutes for overcommitted business unit managers. Without the authority to commit to binding decisions, the SGD teams were stalled—unable to get final agreement on new global work processes. It looked as though the Industrial division's implementation schedule might have to be slipped by a full three months.

Meanwhile, rumors had surfaced within Industrial that middle management bonuses would not be paid this year because of cost overruns on ACCESS-2002. Others said that the SAP product was about to be replaced within Industrial by a less expensive Baan system, and that each business unit would be free to define its own process designs. Project rework caused by the changing of SGD specifications to accommodate Industrial's needs had already generated substantial unpaid overtime for the I/T staff and had generally lowered the energy level of the entire ACCESS-2002 program team. Two SAP specialists (trained during Financials 2000) had resigned recently in frustration—and promptly accepted jobs with more authority and much better pay at other local firms. The vacuum caused by their departure had to be filled by additional and unbudgeted ABC consultants at the rate of $2,500 per person per day. And finally, to compound Cunningham's staffing problems, eight of his best COBOL programmers had left during the spring of 2000 because they perceived a limited future for themselves at GMI.

Dealing with Organizational Resistance
Alerted by the personnel turnover and the slippage in her work
plan, Marilyn Rogers quickly diagnosed what was going on. She
realized that it was time to leverage the support that Brett Berger
had promised. She scheduled a meeting first with Harry Linker
to gain his concurrence.

"Harry, we have a problem in Industrial and it is time to
get Berger involved," she told him. "Some of the line managers
have just begun to realize the size of the commitment required
of them and of their organization over the next two years and
they are experiencing a little 'buyer's regret.' It's surfacing in
missed meetings, foot dragging, second-guessing, and generally
contentious attitudes during project reviews. The key to our
making the due date is to plan-the-work and work-the-plan.
Right now they are resisting us on both counts. This creates extra
work, affects our schedule, and hurts the morale of the team. If
we don't get this drain on our energy under control soon, we are
going to have to adjust either the program scope or our budget.
The completion date can not be rolled back.

"I believe that it is essential at this point for Brett to remind
us why we are putting these new systems into GMI and to reit-
erate his expectations regarding the commitment and participation of his management team. There is a perfect forum for this
at the GMI Management Meeting in three weeks. If we don't do
something about this resistance quickly, the program is going to
grind to a halt."

Linker immediately understood the importance of the trouble that was brewing, and agreed to share her concerns with
Brett Berger. A meeting to air the ACCESS-2002 implementation
problems took place later that week.

Berger was troubled by what he learned. From all prior reports on the progress of ACCESS-2002 he had assumed that the
program was progressing smoothly, and therefore this news
came as an unwelcome surprise. Because his own credibility

with the board of directors depended in part on the success of the program, he wasted no time in confronting the problem. Berger chose to do this by going eyeball-to-eyeball with the most vocal critics of the ACCESS-2002 program during a GMI management retreat held in early September 2000. Here he spelled out in no uncertain terms that, contrary to rumor, ACCESS-2002 was going to go forward as planned. He made it clear that, except for changes mandated by customers or local regulations, there were to be no variances to the standard use of the SAP software and the shared global designs upon which it operated. He reminded his management team that the time to execute this strategic initiative was running short. There was now little more than a year to go on the program; and management bonuses for 2001 would be contingent upon the successful completion of ACCESS-2002. He invited anyone who could not see fit to support the program to find alternative employment.

The open resistance to ACCESS-2002 stopped immediately thereafter. However, Industrial management's objections to the implementation process were never adequately addressed and their discontent with the program lingered.

Your Analysis

1. How well would you say that ACCESS-2002 is proceeding at this point within the Automotive division? To what do you attribute this?
2. How well would you say that the program is proceeding within the Industrial division and why? What could have been done to better manage the situation?

Assessment of ACCESS-2002 Implementation

The implementation of ACCESS-2002 took on two distinct personalities within GMI. In the Automotive division it was embraced as a business solution. In the Industrial division it was shunned as a corporate overhead.

Progress with ACCESS-2002 in the Automotive Division
The implementation phase of ACCESS-2002 went largely as planned within Automotive. A clear business imperative drove the effort forward here, and visible support and active participation by senior management kept it on track. The weekly steering committee meetings in particular played an important role in success by forcing issues of program and project management to be addressed on a regular basis. Changes to a long-term program are incremental. It is essential to keep asking: Where are we now? Has anything changed? What redirection is necessary?

The weekly steering committee meetings provided an opportunity to deal quickly with emerging problems and in particular allowed Marilyn Rogers to move forward with the definition of SGDs. Line managers were uncomfortable that key operating decisions were being made without sufficient analysis, but the process was keeping "the construction project" on schedule. The AUTOLINK deadline of December 2001 was clearly driving ACCESS-2002 within the Automotive division. The Industrial division, however, felt no comparable urgency for change.

Slow Progress with ACCESS-2002 in the Industrial Division
From steering committee reviews of projects within the Industrial division, Marilyn Rogers could see that there was a serious lack of management commitment. Meetings were poorly attended, critical resources were withheld, the implementation schedule was slipping, and key I/T team members had resigned from the company. Many of the changes necessitated by ACCESS-2002 were unwelcome within the division, and clearly line management was not fully on board with the goals of the program. This lack of Industrial management support had to be addressed if ACCESS-2002 was to be completed as scheduled by December 2001.

The problem was simple. From the perspective of Industrial's management, the program's costs were greater than its benefits. They viewed ACCESS-2002 as a corporate program whose goals had been defined not by them but by Harry Linker. Industrial's managers were being told to pay for something they neither needed nor wanted. They saw many of the program changes as unnecessary and others as simply unworkable. They were told to assign their best people to the program on a full-time basis when there was other important work for these people to do. They were told to pay $2,500/day for ABC staff when their own people were available and did not earn that much money in two weeks. And they saw little benefit to be gained from these investments. The project was violating the basic principle of WIIFM (What's in it for me?):

> Everyone whose cooperation a program requires
> must perceive a net benefit or the program will fail.

Most problematic in this regard was the misalignment that existed between GMI's performance measurement system and what its managers were expected to do to achieve the ACCESS-2002 objectives. Specifically, the proposed allocation of program costs would have two negative effects on the Industrial division's RONA. Remember that return-on-net-assets was the basis on which management bonuses were paid. First, nearly $55 million would be added to the "net assets" denominator for this calculation as the program costs were capitalized. Then, starting in 2003, an $11 million expense would reduce the "return" in the numerator each year for five years as this asset was depreciated. Just to stay even, the business units would have to increase revenues by raising prices or driving up volume, or reduce expenses by closing facilities, laying off workers, or cutting materials costs. Each of these operating initiatives would be difficult to accomplish and none of them depended on ACCESS-2002 for success.

Understandably, therefore, Industrial management was trying its best to derail the program or at least to cut it back and slow it down. It attempted to reduce program costs by eliminating program components it felt were unneeded and by substituting Industrial employees for ABC staff whenever possible. These tactics were creating confusion within the program team and disrupting its implementation schedule.

Dysfunctional organizational dynamics will unravel any implementation process and thus break the momentum needed to carry off a large-scale reengineering initiative. It is at a moment like this that an experienced program manager, a detailed work plan, and a strong commitment from executive management are absolutely essential to keeping the program on track. ACCESS-2002 had all three. Marilyn Rogers's detailed work plan quickly alerted her to the slippage in schedule. Her experience enabled her to identify organizational resistance as the cause of the problem. And she successfully called in the CEO to confront the resistance.

Brett Berger's response to the situation, unfortunately, failed to deal with the source of the problem—which lay in the performance objectives that he had established for Industrial's management. His strong actions merely drove the resistance underground. The ACCESS-2002 program was put back on schedule for the moment, but the underlying issue was untouched.

SUMMARY

In this chapter we picked up the GMI-2004 story in September 1999 as the rollout of Financials 2000 was nearing completion two months ahead of schedule. Because this first SAP project was easier than expected, everyone associated with Global Systems 2004 program was optimistic that the projects to follow would also be successful.

But just as the program was about to deploy operational systems into GMI's divisions, strong pressures surfaced to pick up the pace of implementation. Key automotive customers of GMI had just committed to AUTOLINK, a new system scheduled to reach all tier-1 suppliers by January 2002. Although AUTOLINK's requirements would be supported by the new SAP software once completely installed in 2004, none of it would be possible with GMI's current business systems. GMI's automotive customers were unwilling to wait.

This new business pressure pushed GMI management to attempt a dramatic acceleration of their SAP implementation schedule. And CIO Keith Cunningham was forced to abandon his implementation plans for Global Systems 2004 in favor of a more aggressive schedule aimed at bringing critical SAP modules online two years faster than he had originally intended.

Cunningham cautioned against the accelerated schedule, but CEO Brett Berger ignored the advice. Berger viewed the new customer requirements as an opportunity to move forward the benefits promised by GMI-2004. When an independent review of the situation confirmed that an acceleration of the SAP implementation was possible, the decision was made to advance the schedule with a new I/T program called ACCESS-2002.

Marilyn Rogers from ABC-Consulting warned of the risks of too hasty an implementation and observed that the business benefits originally planned for GMI-2004 could not be achieved in the new time frame. CFO Linker understood and yet planned to proceed in any event, with another consulting firm if need be. With a renegotiation in November 1999 of which SAP modules were in and out of the ABC scope of work, Rogers agreed to participate. What had begun in January 1998 as a series of I/T infrastructure investments that were clearly designed to support a new business strategy had now taken on a new purpose. The new scope of work for ACCESS-2002 did not include commitments to business performance objectives; instead, it defined which SAP modules were to be installed. ACCESS-2002 had become a construction project driven by a fixed budget and end date. The program had been cut loose from the strategic business objectives of GMI-2004.

The ACCESS-2002 program began in December 1999 and quickly divided along two paths with differing levels of management support. In the Automotive division it was strongly embraced because it solved the looming AUTOLINK problem. In the Industrial division, however, it was unwelcome because it disrupted ongoing operations and created an unwanted accounting asset and a sizable depreciation expense, while returning little by way of operating benefits. Divisional managers were well aware that the program would make it nearly impossible for them to achieve the financial performance goals corporate had set for them. Implementation faced an unhappy and uncooperative customer.

Through August 2000, the Automotive initiative progressed smoothly, but trouble surfaced in the Industrial division where management openly resisted the program. When alerted to the problem by ABC-Consulting, Berger came down hard on the critics of ACCESS-2002 during a GMI management retreat held in early September 2000. He made it clear that ACCESS-2002 was going to go forward as planned and he invited anyone who did not see fit to support the program to find another job. Open resistance to ACCESS-2002 stopped immediately, but Industrial management's objections to the implementation process were never adequately addressed and their discontent lingered.

Questions for Consideration

1. You have just seen the plan to accelerate Global Systems 2004. What alternative courses of action did Berger, Linker, and Cunningham have?
2. How would you describe the sponsorship situation at this time, vis-à-vis conditions at the start of GMI-2004 in 1997?
3. Do you believe that the GMI management team has seriously considered the business context changes that have occurred since 1997? Are all elements of the organizational infrastructure still aligned with the GMI strategy?
4. What important issues might a one-day meeting focused on the questions in Exhibits 4.1 and 4.2 have raised?

6

Assessing Success and Failure

A s the last chapter ended, we were late in the year 2000. By that time the I/T implementation program ACCESS-2002 had been forced into high gear in pursuit of an essentially unrealistic deadline. In this chapter we jump forward eighteen months to the conclusion of the ACCESS-2002 program in April 2002. From there we reflect back on key events of the intervening year and a half, following the series of incremental decisions that eventually led to the firing of GMI CEO Brett Berger.

■ Wrapping Up the ACCESS-2002 Program

Large change programs tend to take on a momentum and sometimes a life of their own as they extend far beyond their planned
completion dates. Although the final SAP modules for ACCESS-
2002 were successfully installed as scheduled on December 1, 2001,
mop-up work for the program continued on into April 2002. By
that time, Linker was anxious to eliminate the continuing consulting fees, Rogers had moved the bulk of her attention to a new
ERP engagement at another client, and Cunningham was eager
to declare victory and address the many business opportunities
that had been bypassed in the haste of the last two years. Given
GMI's investment in its new ERP platform, the bypassed process-
reengineering opportunities were now ripe for harvesting.

Winding Down (October 2000–April 2002 and Beyond)

The official conclusion of the ACCESS-2002 program for ABC-
Consulting occurred with the sign-off that ABC received on
April 8, 2002—immediately following a formal presentation of
the results of the program to the GMI board of directors. A public celebration for all involved with the program took place on
April 19, 2002, at the end of what appeared to be a record-setting
quarter for GMI operating profits. The dinner brought together
the program team and their spouses in an atmosphere designed
to thank all involved for their dedication and hard work over
the past two years. In addition, the evening was intended to provide an opportunity for team members to say good-bye to one
another, since only a few ABC staffers now remained on site part
time, tying up loose ends for the program. Most of the GMI and
ABC team members had been reassigned and most had already
been redeployed. Brett Berger and Harry Linker (GMI's CEO
and CFO) joined the party briefly to personally express their
gratitude to the team for its efforts.

A well-earned pride in their accomplishment was obvious on the faces of the team members. The required SAP applications had been designed and delivered in phases throughout 2000 and 2001 and the last of these modules had gone online in Hong Kong as planned on December 1, 2001. Parallel operations of the new SAP system and the old COBOL applications had been run during November and December and the entire new system officially went live on January 1, 2002. GMI's books had appeared to close normally at month-end in January, February, and March. With the help of a few renegotiated charges from ABC-Consulting, the program had come in on budget. And, finally, Keith Cunningham and Marilyn Rogers had presented a summary of the program's accomplishments to the board of directors at its April 8th meeting.

As the celebration banquet proceeded, Rogers and Cunningham sat together reflecting on the events of the past three years, and in particular on the rough moments that ACCESS-2002 had had in the Industrial division eighteen months earlier. With valid concerns at that time that the program was being deliberately sabotaged, they had enlisted the support of Brett Berger. Soon thereafter the open resistance to ACCESS-2002 ended. The public complaints and second-guessing stopped; design compromises were negotiated; accommodations were reached; and SGD decisions were at least accepted if not wholeheartedly embraced by the business unit management. From that point on, the program moved forward largely according to schedule.

Some Compromises in Program Scope
As expected, however, some renegotiation of program scope had occurred during implementation. Typical of those changes was the April 2001 decision to abandon the attempt to establish a common customer database with this first release of the SAP software. Largely because the Industrial division was resistant

to any form of real compromise, irreconcilable differences had blocked the installation. The billing and payment conventions in Europe, Asia, and the Americas were different. And it proved impossible to gain consensus on a single workable SGD for handling the variety of order placement conventions and account payment terms that had evolved over time in the regions in which GMI did business. When the impasse was recognized, Rogers had called on Harry Linker to force a decision within forty-eight hours as he'd promised. After two weeks, however, Linker had concluded that because of the company's current contracts with key customers, there would be too much risk to the business to force a single set of transaction terms upon the business units at that time. To proceed prudently, the GMI lawyers would have to be involved to analyze the impact of proposed changes on current contracts and to design appropriate new agreements to be negotiated in the future. Rather than delay ACCESS-2002 pending this analysis, GMI business units would be allowed, for the present, to operate independent order-to-cash processes and therefore to maintain independently formatted files containing customer data.

For the ABC staff, this change of direction in April 2001 was merely a technical challenge. Eight independent customer service interfaces would now have to be written, and in addition a set of data conversion programs would be built around the multiple customer files to support the financial consolidations required by corporate headquarters. These changes generated a significant amount of unbudgeted design and programming work. And as a result, more time and staff would be needed and the budget would have to be increased; or alternatively some existing tasks would have to be removed from the current program scope. Since the end date for the program was fixed for December of that year and a budget increase was politically unacceptable, the only viable option (both for this change and others that would arise later) was to cut back on the scope of the original program. Over time, a variety of reengineering, testing, training, monitoring, and change management tasks were dramatically reduced or dropped from the scope of ABC's work and taken on instead by available GMI staff. Although the work might not be executed with the same level of experience and professionalism, it was expected that it would be performed adequately, and the shift of effort would be sufficient to complete the program within budget.

Declaring Victory for ACCESS-2002

While not everything had proceeded exactly as she'd planned in December 1999, Marilyn Rogers looked back from the celebration on April 19, 2002, with the feeling that ACCESS-2002's core objectives had been achieved and that the program, on the whole, could reasonably be declared a success. As presented to GMI's board of directors, the ACCESS-2002 program had a notable string of accomplishments:

- Delivered complex, state-of-the-art, Internet-ready software on time and within budget
- Established a scalable, flexible, and robust ERP system to support the future growth of GMI
- Built a foundation upon which emerging best practices might be shared on a global basis
- Installed SAP best practices as a basis for some global business processes
- Established ownership of the new SAP systems within both the I/T staff and the user communities
- Institutionalized a disciplined and thorough software design and implementation methodology (that of ABC-Consulting)
- Achieved SAP knowledge transfer to GMI's I/T staff, reducing dependency on consulting firms in the future

- Positioned GMI to harvest planned benefits from a globally integrated information system

The evening's celebration was a testament to these accomplishments.

Accounting Problems Emerge from the New System

The ACCESS-2002 program gave its first public signs of unraveling on the night of the reception held to celebrate its completion. As he left the party, Harry Linker stopped to visit briefly with Cunningham and Rogers. He reiterated his congratulations for a job well done—but then asked both to come to his office for an early meeting on Monday morning. He had just received an urgent call from Tom Judge at A&G, which was still GMI's independent auditing firm. Some of the closing numbers on the latest quarterly financial report looked a little unusual, he said. Linker's staff was likely to need some help from the I/T folks to trace back from the consolidated financials to the underlying business transactions that supported them.

Present at the April 22 meeting with Tom Judge and his team of independent auditors from A&G were Harry Linker, Keith Cunningham, Marilyn Rogers, Ralph Lehman (president of the Industrial division), and his controller Bob Halliday. Tom Judge began the meeting.

"What first caught our eye was an unexplained improvement in gross margin and operating profits within the Industrial division. When we traced the numbers back, working with Bob's folks over the weekend, we found that plant revenues were being booked according to plan, but that labor and material costs were unusually low. With further examination we discovered that variances in plant labor and material were being lost because their associated paperwork was being rejected by the new system.

"As a result you have been booking most of your production for the past quarter at standard cost, which has had the effect of ignoring actual production yield losses. Historically, these losses have run at about 12 percent. In addition, we now believe that a fair number of vendor shipments have been placed into plant inventory and used for production without being recorded into accounts payable because of coding errors made at the receiving docks. Finally, we have uncovered a large and growing suspense file of rejected transactions, which a number of overworked plant accountants have been trying to reconcile by hand during the past two months. Currently, there is at least two weeks of full-time work in that file."

Linker interrupted, "What is the bottom line here, Tom? How bad is this problem? Last week's numbers have already been shared with the audit committee of the board and the street is expecting a positive news release on Wednesday."

"Actually, we are not sure at this moment, but the difference is likely to be material. You have a double whammy working against you here. Both the unbooked payables and the unreported yield losses have understated your cost of goods sold. I am guessing that it will be shy by 10 to 20 percent depending upon the number and size of the payables records in the suspense file. Total impact on the GMI bottom line could be as much as 25 percent. So this is probably not the record-setting quarter that you thought it was last week. It looks now like you are actually below your operating plan for the first three months."

"Damn! Damn! Damn!" muttered Linker. "How could this have happened? If these problems have actually existed for the past three months, how could it be that I did not know about them? How could it be that significant plant charges have been running into a suspense file for three months and no one has taken care of the problem, or at least alerted me to it? Ralph, why have I not been told of this?"

The Search for the Guilty

The Industrial division president, Ralph Lehman, suddenly found himself on the hot seat, but he wasn't planning to be there for long.

"Harry, I assumed that the ACCESS-2002 team would have told us both if there was a significant problem with their new system. While I did know from informal conversations that some SAP transactions were being kicked out for rework at the plants, I have heard nothing about it formally from the program team. I concluded therefore that items in the suspense file were either minor or that they were being resolved in a timely manner by the team. You realize of course that this is not a plant problem; it is an SAP problem."

Bob Halliday, the Industrial controller, took the opportunity to reinforce this point.

"Actually, the plant accounting staff has been pointing out problems to the ACCESS-2002 program team for months now. Even before the December cut-over, plant controllers had warned that the new system was bound to have difficulties. First, it required the use of a whole new coding system for our parts and suppliers. We told the ABC consultants that this had the potential to create operational chaos as labels with the new and old part numbers became mixed and confused. Second, the new software is not compatible with the natural way in which the plants do their work. It is attempting to create new flows of information and new responsibilities. Loading-dock workers, for example, are being asked to perform data entry operations that are clearly clerical in nature. They feel that this isn't part of their job classification and they definitely are not being compensated for the new work. Finally, plant personnel haven't been adequately prepared to operate the new system with the degree of rigor it requires. If you consider that the training for most workers consisted of a single ninety-minute session a week be-

fore the system went live, I'm not surprised that we're still seeing some data entry confusion.

"A typical incident occurred last Tuesday in Cincinnati," controller Halliday continued. "Material for a key monthly production run arrived on schedule, and receiving-dock workers recorded the receipt before placing the material into stock as they were trained to do. The system for some reason rejected the transaction. All needed components were actually sitting in inventory on Wednesday, but the production-scheduling module of SAP refused to release a work order. Since the customer order clearly had to be shipped, the production supervisor performed a workaround by pulling the components from storage and scheduling the work manually. He then carefully documented what he had done and passed his notes on to the ACCESS-2002 program team. He figured they would resolve the software problem and post the necessary data transactions, but it hasn't happened. That item is still in the suspense file waiting for attention.

"Everyone at the plants has realized that what was going on was cumbersome, but we all thought it was working well enough to limp through this transition period, while the I/T staff was working the bugs out of their new system. I personally assumed that if there were any real problems Keith or his team would have told someone."

A Reasonable Plan to Move Forward
Marilyn Rogers quickly recognized that this was going to get messy. She had watched Keith Cunningham's blood pressure climb steadily over the past five minutes as first Lehman and then Halliday had tried to distance themselves from their current operating problems. Although Rogers had been largely removed from ACCESS-2002 during the past two months, spending time on a new client engagement, she believed that both Lehman and Halliday could have and should have known what was going on.

It had been their decision to remove training and conversion preparation from ABC's scope of work. And it had been their staff that had designed and delivered the education that was now being called inadequate. It had been Ralph Lehman specifically who had turned down Cunningham's request to continue four ABC staff members on the program through March 2002 to monitor plant operations for transaction errors and to coach plant personnel with some one-on-one training. Fortunately for ABC, she had been careful to document these decisions in her monthly program reports to the GMI steering committee, just as she had done with several other tough choices that had been made during the past two years. In retrospect, the decisions to move the training and conversion management activities in-house appeared to be penny-wise choices that had come back to bite them.

Rogers could sense that Cunningham was about to weigh in with both fists and the meeting was sure to spiral downward from there. There would be finger-pointing and denials, claims and counter-claims. Everyone would become defensive and the working relationships among these management team members would be irrevocably damaged. She hoped to avoid this fight, at least for the moment.

"Harry, may I say something before we go any further?" she said. "There have been hundreds of discussions held and dozens of choices made during this program over the past two years. And I can understand why at this moment we may have honest differences in our recollections of what things were said, how things were decided, and why things are now happening. On the other hand, I know that we can all agree that our first priority at this moment is to close the books for the first quarter and to file GMI's 10-Q. I propose that we do whatever is needed at this point to get the current problems fixed; we can argue later about who may have been at fault for them."

Linker followed Rogers's lead.

"I agree with you, Marilyn. And therefore this is what I want to happen right now. Since the two weeks needed to clear the suspense file is too long to delay our earnings report, we are going to plan for an announcement next Monday—one week from today. First we will do some triage on those rejected transactions. Tom, anything that your A&G people consider material will be cleared by Saturday morning. The rest of the items can be delayed if necessary. This will give Keith the weekend to rerun the reports. Bob, I want your plant controllers working on nothing but this until it is done. Ralph, I expect that you will authorize the use of overtime if it is needed. Marilyn, if your ABC team can help with the SAP aspects of this problem I would like them involved; specifically, I'd like you to focus on finding and eliminating the sources of these errors. Keep track of your fees and expenses and we can discuss responsibility for this rework and fair compensation later. If anyone discovers that this schedule is going to slip, they should call me immediately. Understood?" All nodded agreement.

"Now, finally," Linker added, "when Berger learned of this problem yesterday, he asked me to organize a team to perform a post-implementation review of the entire ACCESS-2002 program. Some very specific goals for the program were laid out at the meeting in September 1999 when the ACCESS-2002 investment was authorized. On the basis of questions raised by the final report to the board of directors last week, he is now asking for a point-by-point follow-up on the original program plan. Tom, will you make a proposal of how you and your A&G team might be of help to us in this review?"

The meeting then adjourned quickly as Keith Cunningham jotted a note to Marilyn Rogers asking her to stop at his office before she left for the day. He was feeling particularly vulnerable. Harry Linker had not addressed him directly nor even made eye contact during the entire meeting. Harry was obviously displeased. The pending A&G post-implementation review had all of the promise of a witch hunt, and there were already hard feelings between Cunningham and the chief inquisitor. He knew that he was surely the prime candidate for burning at the stake, but he strongly believed that these problems simply were not his fault.

Cunningham needed to vent his frustration over what was happening. He wanted to understand how things could have gone so wrong so quickly. He needed to consider what his options might be at this point, and he particularly valued Marilyn's advice on what he should do next.

Punishment of the (Almost) Innocent

As GMI moved forward after April 2002, the problems in its operating and accounting systems continued to plague its leadership. Despite the best efforts of the GMI management team, it took nearly six months to untangle the mess and to correct the source of the accounting problems. In the meantime, supplier invoices went unpaid, raw materials failed to arrive, production faltered, shipments were missed, and customer accounts lost. Meanwhile, a skittish stock market withdrew from GMI stock and its price drifted downward to less than 60 percent of its value in January 2002. Institutional investors clamored for a change of leadership and a concrete turn-around plan. Brett Berger became the most visible casualty of these events, stepping down on September 5, 2002.

Your Analysis

1. Who do you imagine will emerge as the winners and losers in the post-implementation review? What had they done right or wrong to deserve it?
2. What has occurred between the strong launch of the GMI-2004 in December 1997 and the I/T disasters of April 2002? What were the underlying problems and what signs might have warned of the journey's pending difficulties?

Assessment of the Debacle

As outlined in Exhibit 4.1, a post-implementation review should raise nine pivotal questions. In an effort to determine the success of ACCESS-2002 and to assess the performance of the management team who led it, the following questions need answers:

- Have the performance targets been achieved on time and within budget?
- Are the organization and process infrastructures operating as planned?
- Have the new business capabilities been achieved as described in the business case?
- Has an environment been created in which continuous improvement is likely?
- Are the right measures in place to provide a solid basis for continued value delivery?
- Is the workforce motivated and rewarded for their contribution and performance?
- Has management performance been assessed against business case achievement?
- Are customer needs and expectations being met or exceeded?
- Are the executive sponsors satisfied with the program results?

Who Are the Likely Winners and Losers?
The disappointing facts that will come to light from the answers to the nine questions above will seal Keith Cunningham's fate at GMI. At this point in the GMI story one can predict correctly that his career with the company is over. During the review process that is about to unfold, Cunningham will emerge a loser. He is the natural scapegoat. Whether it was appropriate or not, ACCESS-2002 has come to be viewed within the company as an I/T program and this program has led to a business fiasco. Fair or not, it is now convenient for all involved that Cunningham, as the leader of this I/T program, should depart.

Most tragic here, however, is the fact that this story will have no winners. While the program documentation compiled by Marilyn Rogers will keep ABC-Consulting out of a court-room, the firm is not likely to be invited back to GMI in the near future. Brett Berger himself will be asked to step down as CEO within six months and Harry Linker will not be far behind. Finally, the GMI shareholders come up short in all this, both for the monies spent and the business opportunities lost. Despite the dedication and hard work of hundreds of people and an in-vestment of approximately $240 million on new infrastructure, the ACCESS-2002 program will register in the corporate diary as a failure. In addition, the $2 billion strategic GMI-2004 trans-formation that this program was designed to support has been derailed.

How Did This Happen?

The seeds of destruction were sown into the GMI-2004 journey at the time that Global Systems 2004 was disconnected from its higher purpose of supporting the strategic transformation of GMI and became instead a program to deliver a technology platform. This decoupling from its original objectives would have been clear to anyone who reviewed our model of Journey Management as the program focus shifted in September 1999. At that time, Brett Berger was under pressure from the board to show results from his GMI-2004 initiative. Harry Linker was also fresh from the Fi-nancials 2000 success and confident now that the SAP software was sound and that ABC's project management methodology did indeed work. Since Berger wanted to accelerate the program and Linker thought it was possible, the AUTOLINK mandate was a godsend. It represented the "burning platform" that they could use to drive the organization forward more rapidly. With the date set by GMI's largest customers as a hard target for Internet access by January 1, 2002, it was now clear to everyone that GMI had to convert its information system well ahead of the original schedule. And thus business process changes that were planned for GMI over the next four years would have to be done in two.

Ralph Lehman, the president of the Industrial division, was not convinced, however, since the need for the Industrial division to change to SAP at all was still being argued. Further, Keith Cunningham and Marilyn Rogers both knew that a two-year implementation for the full scope of Global Systems 2004 was simply impossible. This was the moment for all three to speak up.

Ralph Lehman chose to say nothing publicly. Keith Cunningham waited to see how the line managers would react. Marilyn Rogers did engage Harry Linker in an open and frank discussion, stating unequivocally that the original objectives of Global Systems 2004 could not be achieved in the twenty-four months allocated to ACCESS-2002. It would realistically take four years to achieve them. But Linker responded that GMI was prepared to increase the size of the ABC contract substantially while scaling back the scope of deliverables, so that the implementation could be completed in time to meet the AUTOLINK deadline. With that enticement, Rogers got on board.

Brett Berger made an explicit statement of expectations to his management team before signing off on the $106 million price tag for ACCESS-2002. He directed that shared best practices be established across business units whenever possible. At the same time, he locked down the completion date and cost for the program, and he required that the divisions absorb the expense of the program. Linker understood these commitments and assumed that he could force the program forward as he had Financials 2000. Marilyn Rogers, on the other hand, *knew* that she could deliver what *she* had promised, *if* Linker were successful. And if he were not, she could not be held accountable for the resulting problems.

Ralph Lehman's lack of commitment to the program surfaced shortly after the launch of ACCESS-2002. When confronted by Brett Berger, the Industrial division's resistance only appeared to subside. It shifted from public objections to more subtle subversion, such as unwillingness to compromise in the design of the shared global designs. This generated unanticipated requirements and unscheduled work. These changes generated unbudgeted design and programming work by ABC and additional time and staff were needed. Since the end date for the program was constrained by AUTOLINK and the budget had been fixed by Berger, the only viable option was to free resources by reducing scope. Over time, a variety of reengineering, testing, training, monitoring, and change management tasks were dramatically reduced in effort or totally dropped from the ABC contract. These tasks were either declared unessential or taken on by available GMI staff. These changes kept the program within budget, but they also seeded the ground for later problems.

■ The Need for Change Management
and the Collapse of ACCESS-2002

It has been argued that for a business transformation to be successful, a full third of program resources must be devoted to a general activity known as *change management.* Among other things, this activity includes the motivation, training, coaching, monitoring, and handholding of staff during implementation. Its objective is to ensure that new work processes operate as planned and that the benefits of the program are in fact achieved. When pressed for a budget reduction, however, it is tempting to discount the value and need for these activities since they do not produce hard deliverables and are seen as secondary to the design and building of new processes and technology. By analogy, when we travel by plane, we may not see and therefore value the flight procedures that occur before, during, and after the flight. These procedures nevertheless are prudent and essential to ensure control over the success of the journey.

As processes of change management were dropped one by one from her own list of tasks in the GMI engagement, Marilyn Rogers knew that these compromises were creating risk. However, her customer was stating that he was out of money and that he could and would tend to these tasks adequately himself. With the trade-off addressed explicitly and his choice made and documented, the decision was not further challenged nor raised in subsequent steering committee meetings. An atmosphere of "don't ask, don't tell" developed around the issue of workforce preparation, training, and motivation to perform the new operating procedures.

Everyone understood that the preparations for conversion were not ideal, but all believed that the work would be sufficient to complete the program. Once the systems were operational, the team could go back if necessary to address any residual need for training. In any event, frank discussions of possible problems with worker readiness for their new roles and responsibilities failed to become a part of ongoing program management. Eventually, stark evidence did present itself that the operating processes were not working as planned and strong signals indicated the need to stop and rethink the ongoing implementation process. By this point, however, with an obsessive commitment to the established delivery date and no fallback position—that is, without the "Plan B" Cunningham had lobbied for—participants had little choice but to push forward with deployment while mopping up problems as they appeared.

With the budget and end date set, the program had become a race against the calendar to achieve its abbreviated objectives. Because the business case had never been revised to reflect new realities of the program, any efforts to manage management's expectations and to deliver the benefits defined by the original business case had been abandoned. CEO Berger, perhaps to his relief, had been left out of the loop as changes of scope had been negotiated. With no regular and natural process for feedback, he was likely to believe that everything was running smoothly.

At the declared end of the ACCESS-2002 program, GMI did in fact have a tremendous amount of additional work to do. Many business process improvements, organizational changes, and potential benefits had been dropped from the scope of the effort that was to be completed in time for AUTOLINK on January 1, 2002. Moreover, the program had abandoned other tasks during implementation under the pressure of the fixed budget. Yet no explicit consideration was given to work that would be required to achieve the business benefits originally envisioned as part of Global Systems 2004 after ACCESS-2002 was completed. And by the time ACCESS-2002 was completed, the program teams were exhausted, out of money, tired of consultants, and ready to move back to more traditional roles within the company.

■ Why Was ACCESS-2002 Not Halted Sooner?

In the wisdom of hindsight, this question looms large: Why didn't someone halt the ACCESS-2002 program, or at least step in to make significant changes during implementation?

The vagaries of the business environment and the resulting pressures to adjust a company's business plans are not unique to the GMI story. External pressures will surely come to bear on any company during a change program of long duration. And this will make it difficult to sustain effort, discipline, and focus in the light of the outside pressures' disruptive effects on existing journey plans. If left unattended, large programs will lose their way and eventually founder. The general manager must therefore continually monitor changes in the external environment facing the company and assess their impact on current plans and ongoing programs and projects. Management must be prepared to adjust schedules and priorities and even halt programs to ensure that company activities remain aligned with external events and emerging business priorities. In our experience, whenever senior management is unable or unwilling to perform this vital task, monitoring is best done with the assistance of a third party—someone other than the program team or its partners. Someone sufficiently removed from the history of prior decisions and also precluded from future implementation work on this journey. Someone who can be relied upon to sound an alarm when management may need to halt or redirect the program—a knowledgeable yet independent reviewer.

The decision to halt or delay an expensive, long-running program is a very tough call to make and one that can only be taken by senior management. Such programs accumulate baggage during the months and years that they operate. The sweat, energy, and reputation that participants pour into a program can build a strong emotional attachment to it. The decision to terminate the program will imply that a mistake has been made, and people associated with the program will be made defensive. Moreover, when a program is abandoned all costs that have been capitalized to that point must be written off as an expense in the current year, and this may to have a notable impact on the firm's financial performance. Finally, as in the case of GMI, there may be no viable operating alternative available as a fallback position in the event that a problematic program must be aborted or even delayed.

Permitting a dysfunctional program to stumble forward, however, without clear purpose and a reasonable chance of success is an even worse choice to make. Such a decision drains the company of resources and energy and calls into question the quality and professionalism of its management. Since a decision to terminate may have to be made in the future for any program, prudent management demands an investment in contingency planning as part of the preparations for implementation of any large, high-risk, or high-impact initiative.

SUMMARY

This chapter continued our analysis of the GMI-2004 story with a review of key events that occurred between November 2000 and April 2002 as part of the ACCESS-2002 program, which had been disconnected from the higher purpose of supporting the strategic transformation of GMI and had become instead a program to deliver an SAP technology platform. During the eighteen-month period that followed, the program's scope was renegotiated on several occasions as unplanned events unfolded.

This unbudgeted work required additional time and staff from ABC-Consulting, but the end date for the program was fixed and a budget increase was politically unacceptable. To free up the needed resources, the scope of the original program was cut back. Over time, a variety of reengineering, testing, training, monitoring, and change management tasks were eliminated from the scope of ABC's work and taken on instead by less experienced GMI staff.

Marilyn Rogers from ABC understood that these compromises were creating risk. However, her customer was out of money and promising to tend to these tasks adequately himself. Although everyone knew that the transferred work was not being executed with the same level of experience and professionalism, it was expected that it would be adequately performed to complete the program. This assumption proved to be wrong.

The ACCESS-2002 program began to unravel in April 2002 at the end of what appeared to be a record-setting quarter for profit. As independent auditors reviewed preliminary numbers for GMI's first-quarter report, they traced an unexpected improvement in gross margin and operating profits to the Industrial division. Here, unbooked payables and unreported yield losses had understated cost of goods sold and artificially inflated profits. This failure to accurately record manufacturing expenses had inflated the profit guidance provided to financial analysts in March, and profits for the quarter were 35 percent below what Wall Street had expected. Over the six months it took GMI to unsnarl its problems, its stock price dropped more than 40 percent from its January 2002 value. Brett Berger was forced to resign on September 5, 2002.

Questions for Consideration

1. Was it simply a lack of training that led to the misprocessed plant transactions and the havoc they created in the operation of GMI's Industrial plants? Would ACCESS-2002 otherwise have been successful?
2. With the many accomplishments of ACCESS-2002 described to the board of directors in April 2002, how could the program come to be viewed as a failure? How did this list of accomplishments compare to Berger's list of expectations presented earlier in Chapter Five?
3. Can you imagine alternative events that could have occurred during 2000 and 2001 that might have led to a positive ending for the ACCESS-2002 program?

7

Conclusions
and Implications

So there you have it—the saga of GMI has ended in disappointment. Although GMI began well on a journey of strategic change in 1997, with ACCESS-2002 the supporting I/T infrastructure program was caught up in unexpected events and lurched forward on an accelerated schedule driven by an externally imposed deadline. Beginning in December 1999, nearly all journey energies were focused on the I/T program. And because of a fixed budget and a firm completion date, other program support activities were starved to meet these constraints. Consulting services were narrowed, reengineering activities were curtailed, line management concerns were disregarded, and critical accountabilities were overlooked. As a result, the viability of projects, programs, and the entire journey was compromised. The lack of accountability at middle levels of GMI resulted in an escalation of responsibility to higher levels. CEO Berger was of course the responsible party of last resort—he was "the last to know and the first to go."

The facts of the GMI case may seem familiar. As noted earlier, the narrative offers a realistic synthesis of events that we documented in many companies attempting large-scale reorganization in which I/T was a key component. Yet the GMI case remains a work of fiction—any resemblance to real people or events results from the frequency with which we encountered the experiences we describe. Suffice it to say that if you believe that this story is about your own organization, then you are in good company.

We devised the case to end in failure to underscore the true difficulties of such attempts at large-scale change—which may not appear to be so great at the outset as they later prove to be. We composed the case also to make two main points: first, that the Business Architecture and Journey Management models described in Chapter Two are truly of value in describing and managing large-scale corporate change, and second, that there inevitably comes a point at which unforeseen circumstances will challenge any blueprint for change and threaten the best-laid plans.

We will begin this final chapter by discussing briefly how the GMI-2004 outcome might still have been successful, even assuming that the pressure to demonstrate improved operating results forced the sudden jump in schedule. This question will lead us to a discussion of a basic challenge facing leaders of large-scale change. We will conclude with a brief summary of important realities and some corresponding advice.

■ Could the GMI Outcome Have Been Better?

Perhaps the most obvious way that the GMI outcome could have been improved is that the company might have had a better process in place to recognize a significant shift in strategic context. According to our story, CIO Keith Cunningham was first to understand the potential difficulties for GMI-2004 raised by the AUTOLINK requirements. Acting independently, he devised a plan to isolate the effects of the problem so as to leave his existing I/T implementation plans intact. CEO Brett Berger learned of that proposal and of the urgent need to support AUTOLINK only three weeks before the board meeting at which Cunningham's new capital request was to be considered. If Berger and his CFO, Harry Linker, had been in better touch with their automotive customers, they would have informed themselves earlier about the AUTOLINK initiative and GMI's lack of readiness to support it. They could have focused everyone's attention on the AUTOLINK challenge and the pressures that it would bring to bear on GMI-2004. Recognizing the problem sooner, they could have been more thorough in the analysis of their options and the adjustments to the journey plan that would be required.

Another possibility for a better outcome supposes that CEO Berger had chosen to stay more intimately involved in the GMI-2004 initiative from the start. In the case as we described it, Berger largely disconnected himself from the management of the journey, relying instead upon the skills of his newly hired talent (Linker, Cunningham, and Rogers) to manage the details of implementation. Although Berger did get involved to quell insurrections by line managers, he never realized the extent of their opposition—the line managers quickly learned to keep their objections to themselves and their resistance to the journey more subtle. A more productive dialogue might have occurred between Berger and his line managers if he had taken the time to draw forth and help deal with the issues with which they were struggling.

Consider, for example, the confrontation that took place between Berger and Ralph Lehman, the president of the Industrial division, in December 1999 when Lehman learned of the acceleration of the SAP implementation. Recall that Lehman was understandably concerned about the impact that the increased expense and accelerated schedule would have on his division's financial performance. When he challenged the new plan, Berger used his position to demand compliance and Lehman withdrew from further debate. Lehman's subsequent efforts to extend the program and reduce expenses proved disastrous.

As an alternative scenario, we can imagine Berger engaging Lehman in a discussion. Berger would explain the importance of the AUTOLINK customers to GMI, the amount of revenue that they represented, and the clear need to get the operations modules of SAP up and running by January 2002 in order to meet the AUTOLINK demands for online system linkages. In addition he would emphasize the pressure that he was getting from the board for demonstrated improvements in operating performance at a faster pace than the current implementation schedule for GMI-2004.

We can imagine Lehman objecting that AUTOLINK was not Industrial's problem and observing that Industrial leadership would respond badly to ACCESS-2002 in view of the additional costs brought on by an accelerated schedule and its potential impact on their RONA. Out of such a discussion, Lehman might have persuaded Berger to permit Industrial's management team to take another look at the problem and to come up with other alternatives for urgent action to produce the results that Berger demanded.

Reporting back two weeks later, Lehman's team might have proposed an alternative implementation plan. The Industrial division would continue on its current schedule to implement the GMI-2004 programs, while acting immediately to bring forward some of its operating benefits. Industrial management would take control and responsibility for the new plan, which would contain the following key elements:

- Each Industrial operating unit would immediately undertake a process reengineering initiative to deliver the short-term benefits Berger needed. The reengineering might or might not require immediate information system changes. All other information system requests would be temporarily frozen.

- The Industrial division would commit to deliver a net margin improvement of at least 2 percent by December 2000 with a total of 4 percent by December 2001. These savings would be documented, accounted for, and cranked into budgets for performance measurement.

- The principles of shared global designs (SGD) would be adhered to. Industrial would participate actively with Automotive in the design of the new SGDs to assure their usability for Industrial's later conversion to SAP. All potential compatibility issues would be documented and actively worked to resolution.

- At the conclusion of ACCESS-2002 in December 2001, Industrial would launch an operating-unit by operating-unit migration to SAP to be completed by December 2003 at the latest.

This compromise proposal for the SAP program at Industrial would extend over a longer period, involve fewer ABC consultants, and cost less per year for the Industrial division (improving its RONA), but would deliver the profit contribution needed by Berger in 2000 and 2001. Such a process might have preserved the links between the original GMI-2004 concept and its business case while also allowing the Automotive division to meet its AUTOLINK requirements. Essentially, this sort of rethinking could have smoothed out program spending by extending the duration of some projects to reduce the resource impact of others that had to be accomplished by January 2002. The revised plan would have laid the groundwork for explaining the urgency of ACCESS-2002 throughout the company, reengaging sponsorship not only from Lehman but also from the heads of his operating units.

But such a scenario raises a harder question: Is it realistic to expect a CEO to be so intimately involved in managing the details of organizational change, week by week, for months or years on end? It's not as if a CEO has nothing else to do!

■ Is the CEO's Task Simply Too Big?

The GMI-2004 journey was a complex undertaking that depended critically on the success of an I/T infrastructure investment. The growing impatience by CEO Berger for improved operating results forced CIO Cunningham and his staff to scuttle the original implementation plan and substitute a faster one in its place. Unfortunately, Berger treated ACCESS-2002 as simply a somewhat bigger and more expensive software implementation project than the Financials 2000 project that had preceded it, and so he delegated responsibility for it to others. But ACCESS-2002 was different: it would change the jobs, relationships, performance measures, and skill requirements of nearly everyone in GMI.

At what point is the CEO delegating too much? Ultimately the collapse of ACCESS-2002 was triggered by a failure of performance by employees at a very low level in the company hierarchy: Industrial division receiving clerks. When these clerks failed to process material receipts as needed, production controllers were blocked from issuing needed work releases. When plant production faltered, product inventories dried up, shipments were missed, and sales were lost. With lost sales, profits evaporated, the stock price dropped, and Brett Berger got fired. Is all of this to say that, as CEO, Berger should have been down by the loading docks training the clerks? Exactly who *is* responsible for the details of journey implementation activities, such as training the clerks whose jobs will be changed by the introduction of new business processes? Surely it can't be the CEO!

Recurring advice in popular I/T literature asserts that "to assure the success of any important initiative, the CEO should be *actively involved.*" Although strong and active executive support cannot help but improve the chances of success for any I/T program, it is unreasonable to mean by "actively involved" that the CEO must be constantly involved or involved in everything. It is true that executive sponsorship would be a key factor for success in any business initiative, but a single executive cannot be everywhere. At any time in a large corporation there are so many things happening that the CEO simply can not possibly be involved actively with all of them. A CEO can focus on only the most critical issues—the two to five things on which the future of the company depends most. Thus we suggest alternative advice: "To assure the success of a change initiative, the CEO should spend as little time on the program as is necessary, but not less." This subtle shift in perspective forces the consideration of how much executive time is absolutely necessary.

Some tasks unquestionably require the active involvement of the CEO. In Chapter Two we noted that to assure the success of a strategic business transformation, the CEO must first lead a formulation process that will

- Establish the need for change to remain competitive in the emerging world of business.
- Define a shared vision of what the enterprise is to become and how it will get there.

With the purpose established, the CEO must direct the preparation processes that will

- Define the business capabilities required to implement the shared vision.
- Develop a plan to make the investments and implement the actions needed to build the new business capabilities.

With a plan in hand, the CEO must then assure success of the implementation processes that

- Manage the program and project activities necessary to achieve the planned capabilities.
- Harvest the value promised by the strategic vision in a planned and proactive manner.

How deeply should the CEO delve into each of these steps as part of any specific change initiative? The answer depends on the difficulty of the undertaking and the importance of its objectives. The simpler, smaller, clearer, faster, and less important an initiative is, the less essential is active and continuous participation by the CEO. The Financials 2000 project (whose history was described in Chapter Four) provides an example. Disassociate that initiative for the moment from the GMI-2004 journey that it was designed to support, and view it instead as a standalone project whose sole objective was to gather business unit operating results and to assemble them into the corporate financial statements. If the project's goal had been simply to reduce the expense or duration of the existing consolidation process, then CFO Linker and CIO Cunningham controlled all of the resources necessary for success. They would have needed little direct assistance from CEO Berger. On the other hand, because the project was intended to support the new governance processes envisioned as a part of GMI-2004, it was designed to change what operating data was collected, how and when it was measured, and how those measures would be used to reward the performance of line management. It was these effects of Financials 2000 upon the governance infrastructure of GMI that created resistance to the project by line management and eventually required the intervention of Brett Berger to quiet the opposition.

■ Implications for Large-Scale Company Change

Throughout the analysis of the last four chapters, we have offered our insights and certain advice regarding the management problems highlighted there. This section provides a summary of the realities that confront executive management as they lead a business transformation that is heavily dependent upon information technology. The associated advice reiterates key ideas from the book for each phase of the journey.

Reality	Advice
1. Organizations grow comfortable with the status quo and will resist any change that does not exhibit clear and substantial benefits.	As a part of *journey formulation,* gather facts and performance benchmarks that clearly establish the need for change. Set expectations for business performance that are beyond capabilities of the current business processes and infrastructure.
2. A context and vocabulary that enable discussion, understanding, and debate are important for creating and assuring buy-in for a new business vision.	Use the Journey Management and Business Architecture models to provide a framework for discussions. Draw on Figures 1.2 and 1.3 to support an exploration of journey goals and obstacles. Employ a program management and review process to ensure that this dialogue continues through

journey preparation and implementation, and that it occurs in all affected levels and functions of the organization.

3. A strategic vision and an associated business plan are essential to guide tactical and operational decision making. Well-defined business objectives allow everyone in the organization to keep their eyes on the prize while resisting "scope creep" into nice-to-have capabilities that are not required for the business plan.

Define strategic priorities. Create a vision and translate it into concrete goals. Break a broad objective like "Delight the Customer" down into specific measures of achievement and the supporting business process capabilities that are implied. Only then decide which information technology investments must be made to deliver these process capabilities. Summarize the planned benefits in the form of a business case, and thus maintain control over program and project scope and cost.

4. Process reengineering in advance of hardware and software changes may create significant value without substantial I/T infrastructure investment.

Create journey momentum and help funding by concentrating initially on high-visibility projects that yield low-hanging fruit quickly.

5. A CEO's time is scarce, and yet executive involvement is essential for the success of a business transformation.

Consume as little executive time as possible, but no less than is necessary. Executives must get themselves up to speed to understand the journey issues that demand their initial or continued attention. Once the nature and scope of required executive involvement is understood, delegate responsibility and corresponding authority where possible. Use scheduled independent reviews to highlight issues for the CEO.

6. Appearances count. Subordinates within an organization quickly conclude what is truly important by observing where it is that executives allocate their time and attention.

Executive management must be interested observers, visible supporters, informed critics, and demanding sponsors. Establish scheduled reviews and unscheduled inquires to show interest and concern.

7. Speed is of the essence in a journey of strategic change, and yet some organizational change processes take time to unfold effectively.

You need both speed and control at the same time. The management challenge is to keep the two in balance. Create an urgency for change, but be realistic in developing schedules. Proceed as quickly as possible, but no faster than is prudent.

8. The best people will yield the best results, but even

Assign your best and the brightest to journey

the best people will need support as they learn and adapt their skills during the journey.

9. Management decisions will be required for journey trade-offs at three levels: strategic priorities, operational choices, and execution alternatives.

10. Front-end planning and preparation are essential to journey success but also time-consuming and frustrating to managers who just want to get on with the job.

11. Standardized business processes may provide substantial business benefits but may also impose significant organization costs.

formulation, preparation, and implementation. Hire necessary experience or organize a process to build internal capabilities quickly. Ensure competency with required journey management skills. Educate senior management early to increase buy-in. Exhibits 4.1 and 4.2 provide questions that will focus attention on relevant issues and involve managers at all three levels.

During *journey preparation,* focus management discussions on business results. Establish strategic priorities. Build and document consensus. Employ a formal project management methodology to construct a traceable schedule with measurable objectives and intermediate milestones. Make business processes as common as possible, but not more than is practical. Establish standards and tough bureaucratic procedures to review all requests for exceptions, making

12. Success of a large-scale I/T program will not occur without organizational buy-in to both its importance and its linkage to corporate strategy.

13. People will do what they are measured for doing and will resist any change they don't see as in their own best interest.

14. Employees will be reluctant to get involved in a complex change initiative if they view it as high risk and do

them difficult but not impossible to obtain. Accept 80-15-5 process commonality as a realistic goal.

Get all functions and levels of the organization involved and committed to the journey. Pay attention to rumbling that indicates you may not have real buy-in. (Such rumblings are as important as the vibrations that shake a car's steering wheel when the wheels are misaligned.)

Count on people to do what is in their own best interest. Respect the "What's in it for me?" principle. Use performance measures to further the journey. Align measures with intended actions and outcomes. Link management controls and incentives to specific journey objectives (such as revenue, profit, speed, cost, and quality).

Even when people understand and accept the need to change, they will need explanation of their new not understand how they are expected to contribute and where they can find help if they need it.

15. Complex change cannot be totally planned and prepared for in advance. The more complex the undertaking, the less likely it will be that the cost and duration of the journey will have been accurately forecast. The longer the journey, the more likely it will be that unexpected events disrupt the initial plan.

16. The capability to monitor, assess, and adjust the execution of plans is key to delivering success with a journey of long duration.

roles and responsibilities and then training, coaching, and encouragement to move forward to action. You can expect resistance to change during implementation if there is insufficient involvement of employees during preparation.

It is not quite Lewis and Clark exploring the Northwest, but every extended journey has a great deal of uncertainty. Therefore, make the vision and plans as specific as possible, but be prepared to revise them as conditions change and new facts present themselves during implementation. Invest in the option of a "Plan B" whenever the business impact of a program failure would be disastrous. Have contingency plans defined in advance. Remain vigilant and be prepared to execute them.

During *journey implementation*, structure processes of review and decision-making to be fast and transparent. Exhibits 4.1

and 4.2 provide a structure to monitor journey progress and a checklist of questions to assess progress and readiness.

17. The momentum gathered by large programs must be managed to prevent them from hurtling out of control. "Having lost sight of our objective, we redoubled our effort."

Continuous interactive planning and control together with executive tracking and follow-through are critical for journey success. Leverage a formal project management process to track objectives, schedules, and intermediate milestones; provide a regular and recurring review process (a go/no-go checklist); and establish a process to recognize and manage variances to plan.

18. Operating performance will almost certainly decrease at the time of conversion to new business processes.

Anticipate and manage the decline in productivity that will occur during conversion and assure monitoring, coaching, and assistance to recover as quickly as possible. Set up temporary alternative methods to assure critical process performance and control, and be prepared to invoke these alternatives as needed.

19. It isn't over until the business benefits are achieved.

Use the performance
measurement system to
guide and assess imple-
mentation and to certify
accomplishment. Make I/T
program success a regular
item in annual performance
and bonus plans for line
management. Use pay-for-
performance with con-
sultants where possible.
Prevent false declarations
of program completion and
success.

SUMMARY AND CONCLUDING OBSERVATIONS

We began this book by introducing a framework of organizational transformation that places the problems of managing change in a context that
will allow you to address them effectively. The framework consists of two
models. The Business Architecture Model describes five dimensions in
which a business and its operations might change as a result of strategic
choices. The Journey Management Model defines the sequence of activities that must be followed to accomplish such changes effectively. Applying these models as a basis for problem diagnosis and management
prescription, the middle chapters provided details and analysis of the
Global Manufacturing Incorporated story. This final chapter has suggested
an alternative course of action for GMI and offered some principles to
guide a management team as it pursues a complex journey of business
change in the future.

While preparing the GMI case for this book we shared its embed-
ded scenarios with an experienced CEO who dismissed much of the implied advice as basic "Management 101." He argued that any executive
who had successfully reached the level of general manager already knows
this stuff. Such executives know how to build plans, how to manage for

results, and how to sense when a change in journey context has occurred. Over time, he maintained, executives develop an intuition that alerts them to organizational problems and an instinct to ask the right questions to determine when their active involvement is needed.

That's certainly the expectation implicit in the salary and status accorded top management. And yet, virtually every executive we interviewed as part of this study reported being generally disappointed with the results of the major change programs that their otherwise successful corporations had undertaken. Their common lament: "Although we eventually completed the program, we didn't really get the business benefits that we had anticipated!" Perhaps therefore it is not the sophistication of the advice that explains why it is not well applied. Perhaps (like the proven prescription for weight loss—"eat right, eat less, and exercise more") the instructions for success are not hard to understand, they are just difficult to adhere to.

Moreover, not everyone will have good intuition about journey activities with which they have little experience, and it is difficult to apply intuition throughout a multiyear change process involving hundreds of people and tens of millions of dollars. Here change occurs at many levels, locations, and times. Executive intuition is difficult to focus without a clear, regularly adjusted context (Business Architecture Model) and in the absence of a process for forcing frequent reassessments (Journey Management Model). Even then, the intuition of the most capable executive will be worthless without an objective source of factual information. Journey participants may be unwilling to sound an alarm or look for assistance if they fear that alarms are not welcome or that requests for help will be taken as signs of incompetence. And, finally, for our prescription to be effective, there must be an ability and a readiness to change course abruptly when the situation dictates—always an awkward and difficult decision for management to make. It is our belief that by establishing a context and process for ongoing journey assessment, the framework provided here can create an environment in which the task of executive control over I/T system implementation will be successful.

Your own journey may begin here. Let us presume that after reading this book, you believe that there are untapped opportunities for the use of information technology within your company and that you now realize the way to achieve the benefits may be difficult. We are convinced that you will find value in our framework as you proceed through the journey phases of formulation, preparation, and implementation necessary to reach your destination. Thus as you begin, we wish you good fortune and offer the following five questions with which to begin the process within your organization.

Questions for Consideration

1. What are five benchmark examples of I/T-based business strategy that may be relevant to you in your industry?
2. What are your customers, suppliers, and competitors doing in e-business today? How is e-commerce likely to unfold in your industry? Is there a closing window of opportunity for business advantage? A real possibility for a competitive obsolescence?
3. How might your company apply the capabilities of information technology to redesign its products and services, or its processes for design, manufacturing, marketing, and distribution? What is your current plan for the use of information technology in support of business strategy? How does it compare to what might be necessary?
4. What obstacles block your company from making these changes to business processes? What investments in capital, people, and processes are likely to be needed? Who within your organization could lead the journey? What can you do quickly to establish the need for change and thus begin the process?
5. How well prepared is your company to begin a strategic transformation? Specifically, what are your answers to the three indicators of readiness that initiate the process of journey management (as shown in Exhibit 4.1)?

The Authors

Dennis G. Severance received his Ph.D. in computer and communication science from the University of Michigan in 1972. He is now the Accenture Professor of Computer and Information Systems in the University of Michigan Business School, where he has served as chairman of the Computer and Information Systems faculty and director of the Information Systems Executive Forum. Before joining the University of Michigan in 1978, Dr. Severance was an associate professor and principal investigator in the Management Information System Research Center at the University of Minnesota. Prior to that, he was an assistant professor in the Department of Operations Research at Cornell University.

Professor Severance has substantial industrial experience as a member of technical staff with the Bell Telephone Laboratories, as an information systems project officer with the Army Chief of Staff at the Pentagon, and as a senior engineer with General Motors. He has served on the information systems advisory councils of Chrysler, Whirlpool, and General Motors–SPO. He currently acts as an information systems consultant to a number of large corporations and is a member of the board of directors of Tenneco Automotive.

Dr. Severance's current research interests include senior management control of corporate information systems, analysis of long-range information systems requirements for large organizations, enhancement of management decision making through improved information systems, and design of logistics systems for manufacturing and distribution companies. He has lectured in executive development seminars in England, France, Germany, Belgium, Italy, Spain, the Soviet Union, India, Egypt, Singapore, Colombia, Chile, Brazil, Venezuela, Mexico, Canada, and throughout the United States. He has consulted on issues of information technology implementation to over fifty corporations during the past thirty years.

Jacque Passino is the first director to lead Michigan's Department of Information Technology. As part of a bold plan to keep Michigan on the cutting edge of technological change, Passino will lead an effort to unify and manage the information technology functions for the state's nineteen other departments.

Mr. Passino joined the state of Michigan after a brief retirement from Accenture (formerly Andersen Consulting), where he started his consulting experience in 1971 and became a partner in 1981.

Mr. Passino spent the first half of his career in Detroit with Andersen Consulting, where he worked with General Motors, Ford, American Natural Resources, and Domino's Pizza, among others. His expertise includes extensive experience with large-scale change programs, which included global responsibilities in the energy and chemical industry sectors during the 1990s. In the mid-1980s he led the Technology Planning practice, also a global assignment.

Mr. Passino received his undergraduate degree from Duke University in economics and an MBA from the University of Michigan.

Index

B

Baan system, 161

Berger, Brett (fictional), 2–5, 51–63, 65–67, 75, 88, 89, 95, 113, 116, 119, 122, 145–151, 169, 171, 192, 193, 196, 198

Browning, William (fictional), 2, 3

Build and test activities, 53, 114, 117. *See also* Journey management model: implementation phase of

Build the Best People program, 84, 96

Business architecture model, 35–46; and business processes, 44–45; business strategy element of, 38–39; description of, 34; elements of, 36; infrastructure element of, 40–44; performance measurement element of, 39–40; and strategic context element of enterprise, 37–38

Business case, 51. *See also* Strategy definition

Business diagnosis, 49–50; for Global Manufacturing Incorporated, 66–75

Business process changes, implementation of: and assessment of initial progress, 119–120; and building SAP skill base, 113–114; and deployment challenge to financial reporting, 114–116; and financial reporting, 112–113; and importance of regular steering committee meetings, 116–117; and selecting lead projects, 110–118; and third transitional assessment, 108–109

Business processes: five functional systems for operation of, 45; three core, 44–45

Business strategy, 38–39, 50. *See also* Journey management model: strategy definition stage of

Business unit operations: and assessment of move toward logistics and manufacturing systems, 125–126; projects for, 120–126

C

Capability analysis, 52. *See also* Journey management model: preparation phase of

Capability deployment, 53–54, 117. *See also* Journey management model: implementation phase of

CarsDirect, 22, 23

CEO's task, 196–198

Change management, 184–186

Chief operating officer (COO), and current conditions obstacle, 25–27

Cisco Systems, 1; as example of success through I/T investments, 9–10; and improving existing processes between firms, 15–16

COBOL, 171

CommerceOne, 24

Company culture, 37–38

Company legacy, 21–23

Competency, 42

Complete customization, 110

Consumer Federation of America, 23

Consumers Union, 23

Cunningham, Keith, 97–99, 106–107, 109–111, 113, 115, 116, 120, 122, 123, 126, 136–143, 146, 147, 149, 151, 170, 171, 193, 196, 198

Current conditions obstacle, 25–27

D

Delight the Customer initiative, 200

Dell Computer Corporation, 1, 103; as example of success through I/T investments, 7–9; and new practices within firm, 16–17; Premier Page program, 8